········· the ultimate guide to ·········

home
butchering

**HOW TO PREPARE ANY ANIMAL OR BIRD
FOR THE TABLE OR FREEZER**

Monte Burch

Skyhorse Publishing

Skyhorse Publishing books may be purchased in bulk at special discounts for sales promotion, corporate gifts, fund-raising, or educational purposes. Special editions can also be created to specifications. For details, contact the Special Sales Department, Skyhorse Publishing, 307 West 36th Street, 11th Floor, New York, NY 10018 or info@skyhorsepublishing.com.

Skyhorse® and Skyhorse Publishing® are registered trademarks of Skyhorse Publishing, Inc.®, a Delaware corporation.

Visit our website at www.skyhorsepublishing.com.

10 9 8

Library of Congress Cataloging-in-Publication Data is available on file.

Print ISBN: 978-1-5107-4601-5
Ebook ISBN: 978-1-62914-269-2

Printed in China

Contents

the ultimate guide to
home
butchering

Introduction

Why Butcher
Your Own?

IN DAYS PAST, butchering your own food was a necessity. Eating meat required killing and processing the animal. Today home butchering is more a choice than a necessity. Most people that choose to butcher at home do so for a number of reasons, with control over the food they eat the most important reason.

Continuing problems with commercially butchered meats are a great concern with many. If you do your own butchering, you know how safely the meat was prepared. If you raise your own animals and

LEFT: In days past, home butchering was a necessity for many, and a regular event on farms such as the Burch farm back in the '40s.

then butcher them yourself, you have the ultimate control over the meats you consume. You control not only the safe processing, but also the quality and type of meats consumed.

Another reason is cost. Home butchering saves money. The third reason, and one growing in popularity, is the self-satisfaction achieved in doing it yourself, a definite step to more self-reliance.

If you're a hunter, especially of deer and big game, do-it-yourself butchering should be an important component of the hunt. Knowing how to properly field dress and cut up wild game is invaluable.

Although the killing is not pleasant, cutting up meat is a rewarding and enjoyable task for many, and a valuable, easily learned skill. While learning, you can usually "eat your mistakes." Although I have been involved in butchering hogs from an early age, when I faced my first beef I was a bit daunted by all the different cuts. "Doesn't matter," my wife Joan said, "It all eats." And, it does.

Like many old-time, once-invaluable life skills, home butchering has been lost to many through the last few generations. Our family has been home butchering for many generations, and we each learned from our elders. This mentoring was invaluable. Most people

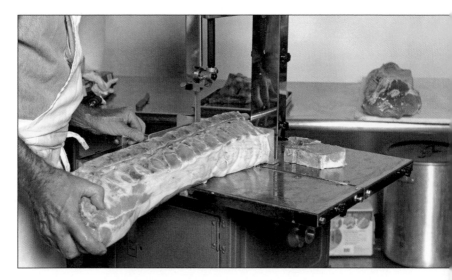

ABOVE: Home butchering allows you to have control over the quality and safety of the meat you eat.

ABOVE: If you hunt deer and other big game, knowing how to field dress and cut up your game is an extremely important skill.

ABOVE: Home butchering is an easily learned skill, and a great way of adding to your independence and self-sufficiency.

today don't have the opportunity to learn such life skills at the side of an experienced butcher, but the skills are not hard to learn, and hopefully this book will provide you with the knowledge needed and the incentive to do your own home butchering.

LEFT: The author in the '50s with his first litter of pigs. As a do-it-yourself butcher, you can save a great deal of money and, if you raise your own livestock, have even more control over your food.

① Tools and Supplies

BUTCHERING CAN BE done with nothing more than a sharp knife. Our ancestors butchered with a sharp piece of stone. Modern knives and tools, however, make the chores easier, faster, and safer. The number and type of tools needed depends on your butchering needs. For instance, if you plan to butcher just a chicken or two, you'll need much less equipment than for slaughtering and cutting up a steer. Some tools you may already have in your kitchen or garage. Some

LEFT: The number and variety of tools needed for butchering depends on how often and how much you butcher, as well as what types of animals.

tools are more specialized, and some tools used in the past may no longer be needed. I was lucky to not only be mentored in butchering, but also to have inherited a number of tools. Some of those, however, are now more valuable as antiques, yet some are still quite valuable butchering tools. With the growing interest in self-sufficiency, more people are home butchering, and more companies are offering tools for the home butcher. A number of companies offer butchering tools and supplies online.

General Tools

Some tools can be used for butchering of all types. Other tools are for specific butchering chores.

Knives

Knives are the most important butchering tools. Purchase only good-quality knives. They will more easily sharpen, stay sharp longer, and do the job easier and safer. Good-quality knives can last your lifetime and then some. I have some handed-down knives that are now being used by the fourth generation. The quality and type of steel in some of today's knives, however, is different than in the

BELOW: Good-quality knives are the most important tools for butchering. A variety of knives, including skinning, boning, and meat cutting, makes the chores easier and safer.

really old knives. Most butcher knife blades are made of three different types of steel: carbon, stainless, and high-carbon stainless steel. The older knives were primarily made of simple carbon steel. Carbon steel is relatively soft and sharpens very easily, even with nothing more than a handheld stone. It doesn't, however, hold an edge very well and must be continually sharpened. Carbon steel also rusts badly, even if the metal is dried after cleaning. One solution is to coat the metal with a light dusting of cooking oil spray before storage. Always wash the knife thoroughly before using to remove any residual oil and/or rust. Pure stainless steel is the hardest of the three metals; it will hold an edge longer and will not rust. It's extremely difficult, however, to properly sharpen a stainless steel knife. The majority of the quality butcher knife blades today are made of high-carbon stainless steel. This material provides the best of all worlds: an easily sharpened blade that will hold an edge a reasonable amount of time, yet doesn't rust as readily as carbon steel. A variety of handle shapes and materials are also used in knife construction. In quality knives the handles will be most commonly made of hardwood or a synthetic material. The latter, sometimes made of soft-molded materials, are easy on the hands for long periods of use.

Butcher knife blades are commonly ground into one of three shapes: flat, hollow, or taper. Flat-ground blades have their edge ground evenly from the back of the blade to the front and from the heel to the point. These blades are sturdy and easily sharpened. Hollow-ground edges have a portion of the blade just behind the edge thinned. This design creates less drag, but it also creates a weak area in the blade. A better solution is the taper-ground knife. In this case, after the flat grind, an additional grind is made to thin down the blade, but not to the thinness of a hollow-ground edge. A taper-ground edge produces a knife with less drag, but is stronger than hollow-ground edges, and is only found on high-quality knives.

Most people associate the early settlers, trappers, explorers, fur traders and others who opened our country with a big "Bowie" hunting knife. And for the most part they only had one knife, but typically it was often a "Green River" butcher knife—a six- to eight-inch curved-blade skinning knife that was sturdy, easily sharpened, and multipurpose. The knife was used for skinning, butchering, camp chores, and for self-protection when needed. You can do all the butcher chores with a similar knife. Having more than one knife suited for different chores, however, makes home butchering easier and more efficient. I have two or three of some types of knives so that I can simply pick up a sharp knife and continue working rather than stopping to sharpen. Multiple knives are especially helpful when skinning, which can quickly dull their blades.

The different types of knives vary in blade shapes. For instance skinning knives are relatively short, with a rounded drop-point. This helps prevent the point from sticking into the meat during the skinning process. If you field dress deer and other big game, a short, drop-point skinning knife with a gut hook can be invaluable. You can of course use a skinning knife for cutting up the carcass, but regular butcher knives with long blades are best for this chore. Butcher knives also come in a wide variety of sizes and shapes. Long-bladed butcher knives are best for the initial carcass sectioning, slicing meat, and cutting meat into chunks for grinding. I prefer the rounded-tip butcher knives rather than those with a sharp tip for cutting meat into smaller pieces. The upswept tip doesn't catch on meat as you slice it. Boning knives with their thin, flexible blades are best for boning out meat.

Sharpeners

Keeping knife blades sharp is an extremely important facet of any type of meat preparation. Using the proper tools can make it easy to have sharp knives as needed. Knife sharpening devices are widely available, ranging from the simple, but extremely effective, butcher's steel to powered sharpeners. Knives that are in good shape but dull should never be sharpened using a powered grinder, as you could overheat the steel and lose the temper. Powered sharpening hones, however, can make the chore of sharpening a dull knife

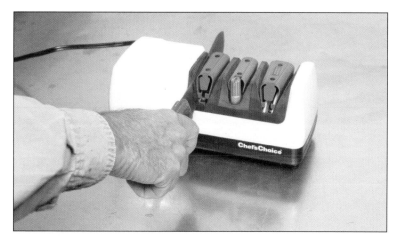

ABOVE: A means of keeping knives sharp is also important. An electric sharpener, such as this Chef'sChoice, makes the chore quick and easy.

quick and easy. I've tested the Chef'sChoice models for many years. The Chef'sChoice Model 130 Professional Sharpening Station is an excellent choice. It will sharpen both straight and serrated edges and has a 125-watt motor with three sharpening stages: 40-degree pre-sharpening, 45-degree sharpening, and a third steeling stage for final honing. A number of other models are also available.

BELOW: A handheld butcher's steel or diamond sharpener can be kept near your cutting table or skinning area for a quick touch-up of the blades.

One hand-sharpening system I like is the Lansky Sharpening System. The kit contains finger-grooved hone holders that are color coded for easy identification of the exact sharpening angles desired. The kit includes a carrying case, a knife clamp with angle selector, guide rods, extra attachment screws, oil, and a sharpening guide. Depending on the kit selected, a variety of coarse, medium, and fine hones are available. You should have either a butcher's steel or a "hand-hone" readily at hand where you are working as you'll continually need to "touch up" the blades as you work.

Saws

A handheld butcher's saw is necessary for quartering and cutting up pork, beef, venison, and other large carcasses. These saws utilize a removable, easily cleaned blade with very fine teeth. The saws are available in several sizes. If quartering and cutting up a

RIGHT: A powered meat bandsaw makes the chore of cutting steaks, chops, and roasts easier and more precise.

BELOW: A hand meat saw is necessary for many chores, such as quartering larger animals, trimming hams, and cutting loins into chops.

beef, you'll need a saw of at least twenty-four inches in length. This type of saw is awkward at best for cutting individual bone-in pieces such as steaks, chops, and ribs. It will work, but a powered butcher's bandsaw is the best choice. These power saws are fairly expensive, but are a good investment if you annually butcher large animals, such as beef, from which a lot of steaks and other bone-in pieces are cut. You can, of course, debone any carcass and remove the bones as well as the expense of a powered saw. Deboning also saves on freezer space.

For years our family hand sawed only what was necessary: on pork, for instance, we removed the loins from the backbone, instead of cutting into bone-in pork chops. Most of these electric-powered saws also come with a built-in grinder which makes them a good value.

Meat Grinders

Many meats, or cuts of meat, are best ground into sausage and hamburger, including beef, pork, venison, and even lamb. Chicken and turkey can also be ground into lean, healthful meats. If you're only grinding a small amount of meat, a hand-grinder will do. They

BELOW: If you grind meat into sausage or hamburger, you'll need a meat grinder. A hand-cranked grinder is the most economical for small jobs.

For larger meat grinding chores, a powered grinder is best. These are available in a wide variety of sizes, depending on the motor size. The unit shown is capable of grinding 360 pounds of meat per hour.

will, of course, grind only as fast as you can crank by hand, and they do require muscle power. Many of these hand-crank grinders can be found in antique shops and flea markets, often at bargain prices. If you buy them secondhand, you should make sure all parts are there and you will probably need to sharpen the blade and plate. Sharpen the plate by running it across a fine hone, holding it down flat on the hone. Use a file to remove any nicks and sharpen the blade, then hone the edges sharp. You can also purchase new hand-crank food grinders, just like our grandfathers used, but made with modern materials. They're available in both bolt-down and clamp-on models, in tinned or stainless steel. The latter are more expensive, but easier to clean. The newer models come with larger clamps so they more readily clamp to almost any countertop or tabletop. Most grinders come with a coarse plate and a fine plate, and a set of three stuffing tubes. The larger grinders can grind around five to six pounds per minute with enough muscle power.

For many years, I used a large, antique, electric-powered grinder I inherited from my granddad. It had a huge flywheel and was powered by a big electric motor with a belt. My granddad originally powered it with his Model A automobile, jacking up the rear wheels and running the grinder with a giant belt. The throat opening is large and the grinder didn't come with a safety pusher as do today's powered

BELOW: Many home-model meat bandsaws also come with a meat grinder attachment.

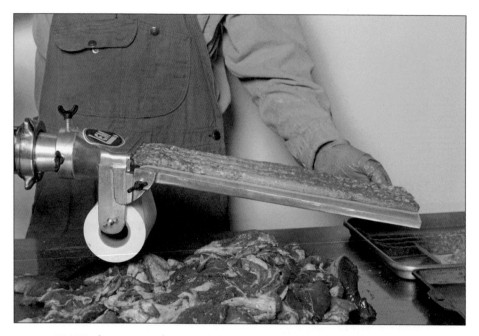

ABOVE: Accessories such as ground-meat patty makers and jerky and sausage stick makers are available for some grinders.

grinders. It was and still is dangerous, not only the grinder, but also the spinning, flopping belt and old nongrounded electric motor, but our family used it for three generations.

The ultimate meat grinder is an electric-powered model, and if you do a lot of meat grinding you'll be sure to get your money's worth. Some of the larger, powered butcher tools can be quite an investment, but they're usually a lifetime investment, with little loss in value. You might also wish to do as the old-timers did and pool your resources with family and friends. In the old days when families worked together on butchering, one family might own the grinder, another a lard press and kettle, and so on. Electric-powered meat grinders are available in a number of sizes, depending on the horsepower, which determines the amount of meat that can be ground in an hour. Smaller models will do the job, but with less power they are slower.

For the most part, however, you're not trying to beat the clock. I've owned and used a number of grinder models and my favorite is a

ABOVE: You'll need a sausage stuffer for making sausages. Most grinders come with sausage-stuffing tubes, making it a one-step operation.

Bass Pro/LEM No. 12. It features a .75 horsepower motor and is capable of grinding 360 pounds of meat per hour.

The grinder has a heavy-duty, stainless steel construction with an easily cleaned housing, grinder head and auger, a permanently lubricated motor, built-in circuit breaker, all metal gears, heavy-duty meat pan, meat stamper, stainless steel grinding knife, one coarse and one fine stainless steel stuffing plate, and three stuffing tubes.

Similar-quality models are available from a number of sources. Some grinders also have a variety of accessories that can be used with the grinders, including: tenderizer attachments, ground-meat jerky and snack-stick makers and ground-meat patty makers.

Sausage Stuffers

In most instances of small batches of sausage, you can simply use the sausage-stuffing tubes with meat grinders. You may, however, wish to use a dedicated sausage stuffer for larger volumes or for stuffing highly emulsified meats, such as bologna and hot dogs. Grinding and stuffing at the same time can be a problem with these products. Sausage stuffers are available in several forms including a simple, plunge-type hand stuffer. These consist of a tube with a plunger and a stuffing tube on one end. They're the least expensive, but fairly hard to operate and they don't produce consistent sausages. The next step up is a lever-operated stuffer. These consist of a cast-iron L-shaped tube and a lever to push a plunger down through the tube. As I discovered years ago, older models allowed a lot of sausage to escape back past the plunger due to back pressure from the sausage. Newer models have a rubber or plastic gasket to help prevent this leakage problem around the plunger. Vertical stuffers are the easiest to use with the least amount of hassle and produce more consistently shaped sausages, especially when stuffing smaller diameter casings. Vertical

BELOW: Dedicated stuffers, such as the vertical model shown, are easy to use and can produce a larger quantity of sausage quicker. These stuffers are necessary for finely ground processed meats, such as bologna and summer sausage.

stuffers are made in several sizes, ranging from five- up to twenty-five-pound capacities. All are made of stainless steel and the cylinder removes for easy cleaning. A variety of different size stuffing tubes comes standard with most models. Complete sausage-making kits, including stuffers and spices, cures and casings are available and a great way of getting into sausage making. For more information on sausage making, see my book *The Complete Guide to Sausage Making*.

Miscellaneous

Other items include tubs and plastic pans to hold meat, lots of clean cloths, paper towels, food-safe gloves, kitchen scales, hanging scales, kitchen thermometers, measuring cups, cutting boards, and meat tenderizers. A powered meat slicer can also be a great help. A vacuum-packing machine will help keep meat fresher longer in the freezer. And, you'll need a good home freezer. Other supplies include freezer paper, plastic food wrap, vacuum bags, freezer sheets, rubber meat stamps, wrapping tape, and hamburger bags. You may also need cures, salt, pepper, and spices for jerky,

BELOW: You'll also need lots of miscellaneous items including tools and supplies such as freezer paper, tape, plastic wrap, and so forth.

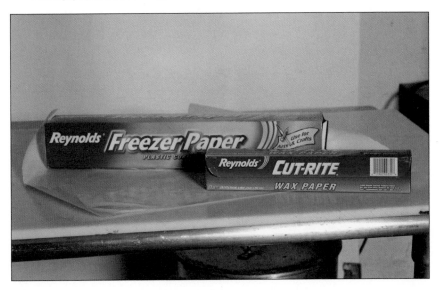

sausage, and salt cured/ smoked meats. If you really get into jerky and sausage making and salt/ smoking, you'll probably want a dehydrator and smoker.

Specialty Tools

Some butchering, such as hog scalding and butchering a beef, also requires specialty items. Butchering poultry is easier with a killing funnel.

Chicken plucking can be done using an old canner or similar pot and a fish fryer for heat. A pair of sturdy kitchen shears makes splitting chicken carcasses easier.

To scald a hog you'll need a scalding tank, usually a fifty-gallon steel

ABOVE: Different types of butchering also require specialized tools. For poultry you'll need a killing funnel that you can easily make from a plastic bucket.

BELOW LEFT: You'll also need some means of scalding the birds for plucking. A fish-fryer burner and an old boiling-water bath canner works well.

BELOW RIGHT: Heavy-duty poultry shears or kitchen shears are necessary for splitting poultry.

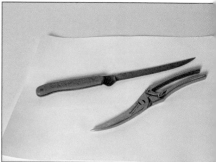

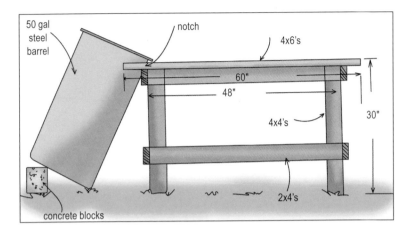

ABOVE: If you scrape hogs in the old-fashioned way you'll need a scalding tank, a sturdy table, and a bell scraper.

drum; a table on which to place the pig after the scalding tank; and a block and tackle to hoist the animal for scalding or skinning, and gutting. A tractor with a bucket is a very handy tool.

A meat pole can be used to hold the block and tackle and hog or beef.

BELOW: A meat pole is extremely handy for hanging game and larger carcasses.

ABOVE: Butchering larger animals such as hogs and cattle requires a heavy-duty gambrel and some means of hoisting the carcass.

The old-timers used a "single-tree," a piece of horse harness hitch that spread the legs apart to lift the carcass. A heavy-duty gambrel is the most common choice these days. A pritch pole about 2.5 feet long is needed to prop up a beef carcass. Make sure the meat pole, block and tackle, and gambrel are extremely sturdy for working with a beef carcass. A hay hook or similar handled hook is necessary for lifting the hog in and out of the scalding water. You'll also need bell scrapers to scrape the hair from the hog. These are available new from butcher supply sources, but can quite often be found in antique shops and flea markets. If you intend to use the whole hog and render the lard, a lard kettle and lard press may be in order. Again, these old-time items may be hard to come by, and lard presses are not cheap, even when you find them. You can also render lard over a fish-fryer base with an old canner or other large pot. A turkey fryer works great for the chore. A stunning hammer or .22 rifle is necessary for killing hogs, beef, and other larger animals.

ABOVE: You'll need a comfortable place to work, in most instances, both outside and inside. The outside area is used for killing, skinning, gutting, and hanging.

BELOW: The inside work space is used for cutting up the carcasses, making sausage, grinding meat, wrapping and packaging, and other chores.

ABOVE: A table of the correct working height for you is important. It should also be sturdy enough to hold the weight of larger carcass quarters, and the surface must be easily cleanable.

Workplace

You'll need a comfortable, safe place to work. If just doing a chicken or two you can do some of the work in your kitchen, but you'll still need an outside work table. The old-timers usually had a special place set aside for these butchering chores, often with the tools stored nearby. Most home butchering is done in cold weather, and you'll need protection from the weather for some of the chores. An open-sided shed is ideal. An unheated garage is often the choice of many.

The main requirement is plenty of water. If you don't have running water to the site, you should be able to have a hose or carry buckets easily to the site.

In addition to a table for scalding, an easily cleaned table is necessary for cutting up meat. You can do some small chores on your kitchen countertop, but cutting up a hog or beef half requires a good-sized and sturdy table.

The tabletop should also be nonporous, and easily cleanable. A number of years ago, I purchased a pair of stainless steel tables at a

ABOVE: Easily cleaned cutting boards are also necessary.

school auction. These are ideal as they can be cleaned and sanitized. Quite often going-out-of-business restaurants will also have these for sale.

In lieu of the ultimate table, a large, synthetic cutting board is the next option. Smaller, kitchen-sized cutting boards are also handy. Regardless of what is used, it must be easy to clean and sanitize.

② Food Safety

ANY TYPE OF food processing, including butchering, requires an understanding of safety issues and careful adherence to safe food-handling methods. This includes utilizing safe foods, such as disease-free meat, safe food-handling steps, and safe food processing and preservation. Home butchering, however, is not all that complicated, and is perfectly safe if you follow the necessary safety methods.

BELOW: Food safety is extremely important in any food processing and especially so in butchering.

Safe Meat

The first prerequisite is safe meat. Meat should only be used from healthy, disease-free animals, and that's where the home butcher has the advantage. If you're raising your own animals and poultry for food, you'll know if they're healthy. Do not butcher sick animals. It's also especially important to make sure purchased animals and poultry to be butchered are healthy and safe to eat. Pasture-raised beef, pork, and even chickens produce safer and healthier meat. It's important to be aware of diseases such as CWD (chronic wasting disease), found in deer, elk, and moose; and BSE (bovine spongiform encephalopathy), an extremely rare problem found in beef cattle, as well as the parasitic diseases such as trichinosis in hogs, bear, and some other wild game.

BELOW: First requirement is to butcher only healthy animals and birds. Those that are sick must not be butchered. If you have any questions, you might consider checking with your local veterinarian.

CWD is a concern with some deer and elk hunters. According to the Wildlife Management Institute:

There is currently no evidence that CWD is transmissible to humans. However, public health officials recommend that human exposure to the CWD agent be avoided as they continue to research the disease. Although the agent that causes CWD has not been positively identified, strong evidence suggests that prions are responsible. Prions are abnormally shaped proteins that are not destroyed by cooking. Accordingly, hunters are advised not to eat meat from animals known to be infected with CWD. Research completed to date indicates that prions generally accumulate in certain parts of infected animals—the brain, eyes, spinal cord, lymph nodes, tonsils and spleen. Based on these findings, hunters in CWD areas are advised to completely bone out harvested cervids in the field and not consume those parts of the animal where prions likely accumulate. Health officials advise hunters not to shoot, handle or consume any animal that is acting abnormally or appears sick. In addition, they suggest hunters take normal, simple precautions when field dressing a carcass. A complete list of current hunter recommendations is available at www.CWD-info.org.

A number of years ago I started completely boning out the deer we killed. This was not due to CWD, but the fact I could store a lot more meat in the freezer off the bone, than on, and boning out the meat made a big difference in the amount of food one freezer would hold for a family of five. Basically, you end up with an entire deer carcass including skin attached to the head and all the meat removed. The chapter on butchering wild game illustrates the technique.

Parasitic diseases can also be a problem. Toxoplasmosis is a parasitic infection caused by the protozoan known as Toxoplasma gondii. Humans most often become infected by this organism by consuming undercooked meat, especially lamb, pork and venison—or eating unwashed fruits and vegetables. Cats, both domestic and wild, are often the carriers. A healthy person who becomes infected often experiences few symptoms, but people who have weakened immune systems are at risk of severe complications.

Trichinosis or trichinellosis is a disease caused by the parasite called Trichinella. According to the Centers for Disease Control and Prevention, National Center for Infectious Diseases, Division of Parasitic Diseases:

Trichinella species have been found in virtually all warm-blooded animals. It's important to avoid eating undercooked meat of pork, bear, cougar, wild boar and walrus. Make sure the meat is cooked to an internal temperature of 160 degrees F. before consumption. In the past, it was thought freezing for 30 days or more killed the parasite, but trichinella in meat is often not killed by freezing and some home freezers will not reach the temperatures needed to kill parasites. Commercial irradiation is used to kill the parasite. Smoking, drying, curing or microwaving does not consistently kill the infective trichinella worms.

Hogs can also carry diseases transmittable to humans, including leptospirosis or "lepto." In most cases farm-raised pigs that are healthy when butchered do not cause a problem, but wild hogs that are killed while hunting can be a problem. Rubber gloves should be worn while handling or butchering these animals.

Rabbits can also carry rabbit fever or tularemia, which is more commonly found in wild rabbits. The bacteria are present on a rabbit's fur and in internal organs and body fluids. The bacteria are destroyed by cooking, so the only way tularemia can be contracted is by handling. The bacteria do not enter healthy skin, but can infect humans through cuts or scratches. Rubber gloves should always be worn when dressing rabbits.

Safe Processing

It is also extremely important to safely process meat. Meat that is tainted, unsafely butchered, and cut up poses serious health prob-

ABOVE: Use all safety precautions when dealing with wild game that might have diseases, including wearing food-safe gloves when field dressing, skinning, and gutting.

lems, especially from E. coli. As a kid back in the '40s, I watched the community butchering processes as neighbors and family worked to butcher hogs. My dad often told the story about a mishap when a piece of meat fell off the cutting table only to drop on the ground where the hog scalding and scraping had occurred and was covered with hair. "One that eats the most sausage gets the most hair," a neighbor joked as the scrap was quickly eaten by the neighbor's dog. Food poisoning by tainted meat, however, is no joke. The most common cause is E. coli, a serious and deadly health problem. E. coli is a bacterium that commonly lives in the intestines of people and animals. Many strains of E. coli exist, though most are normal inhabitants of the small intestines and colon, and are nonpathogenic. This means they do not cause disease in the intestines. E. coli 0157.H7, however, is a dangerous disease-causing bacterium coming mostly from poorly cooked meat, usually hamburger—the reason why the disease is often called "hamburger disease." E. coli causes bloody diarrhea, cramps, and kidney disease in children. The most common cause of the disease is contamination of the meat from intestinal fluids, spilled or smeared on the meat during field dressing or butchering. This is especially so when the meat is then ground, causing the contamination to spread throughout the meat. Make sure all meat is properly handled and cooked to the proper temperature for the different types of meat.

Field Dressing and Gutting

Most E. coli health problems are caused during the field dressing of wild game and gutting of domestic livestock. There is no reason you shouldn't do your own meat processing—it's not complicated and food safety is not an issue if you follow common sense safety rules. Use the proper steps in field dressing and caring for the carcass and then make sure the meat is processed properly. If you process your own meat, including wild game, you will know exactly what you and your family are eating. Field dress wild game and gut domestic livestock as soon as possible after they have been killed to allow body heat to quickly dissipate. Venison and other wild game shot while hunting can be heavily contaminated with fecal bacteria—the degree varying with the hunter's skill, location of the wound, and other factors.

During field dressing, take all necessary steps to avoid puncturing the digestive tract, a common problem caused by not cutting around and tying off the anus, or cutting into the intestines when opening the abdominal cavity. A sharp, gut-hook knife helps solve the problem. With a gut-shot animal, however, you'll have a problem. Sometimes this can't be avoided, and while guiding deer hunters, I've dressed more than one gut-shot deer. It's not pleasant. Remove

ABOVE: Meat must be safely processed through each step. The first step is during the field dressing or gutting. Take care to avoid cutting into the intestines, spilling fecal matter and contaminating the meat.

as much digestive material as possible and thoroughly wash out the cavity with lots of running water. Then cut away and discard any meat that has been tainted. Thoroughly clean and disinfect the knife and any other tools before further use. Discard rubber gloves.

Aging

Deer and other big game, as well as beef, is usually aged. Pork is never aged, nor is lamb or goat. If the weather stays suitable, you can skin and hang the carcass for a few days, but the temperature should not reach above 45°F. If the temperature drops below freezing, the aging is slowed. Fresh beef at the slaughterhouse is rapidly chilled down to 40°F, and then aged at that temperature for seven to ten days. The home butcher must depend on the weather for aging deer and beef carcasses, and since these are usually held at ambient

ABOVE: Fresh butchered meat must be chilled as quickly as possible to below 40°F. Larger animals should only be butchered when there is consistently cold weather; chickens and small animal meat can be quickly chilled in ice water.

temperatures, there is a possibility for bacteria multiplication. Some prefer to allow the carcass to hang for a few days, then skin just before quartering and butchering. This does prevent the surface of the meat from drying out, but it takes longer to achieve the initial chill. If you

BELOW: Carcasses such as venison and beef benefit from aging by hanging. This must, however, be done in suitable temperatures of 32°F to 35°F.

have an old refrigerator, set the temperature to 35°F to 40°F, cut the carcass into quarters, and age the meat in the refrigerator for about a week. This will work on a small deer, but not a larger carcass. Blood will pool on the lower ends, so make sure you place the pieces upright in pans and drain away the excess blood daily.

In any case, chill the meat to below 40°F as quickly as possible to minimize contamination problems. Fresh butchered poultry and small animals can be placed in ice water to chill immediately. Butchering of larger animals must be done in cool or cold weather. It takes from twelve to fifteen hours to chill a 150-pound hog carcass down to 40°F with refrigeration or ambient air temperatures of 32°F to 35°F. Continuous exposure to freezing weather, however, causes problems with uneven chilling. It is not unusual for our family and friends to have a half-dozen deer down on opening day, and here in the Ozarks the daytime temperature during November can often be in the 70s. Several years ago I found an old "reefer" or refrigerator truck body that a going-out-of-business restaurant wanted to get rid of. For a couple hundred bucks and a little help from a friend with a flatbed trailer we acquired a giant walk-in cooler. In warm weather we use the unit to hang deer to age, as well as to hold quantities of meat in covered tubs while we process it.

Cleaning and Disinfecting

One of the most important facets of all steps in butchering and meat processing is to keep everything clean and disinfected. This includes work surfaces such as tables, countertops, and cutting boards. Make sure to thoroughly clean and disinfect knives, grinders, stuffers, meat saws, and any other tools that come in contact with

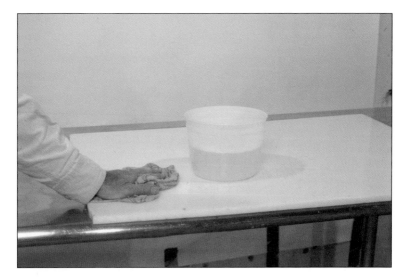

ABOVE: When it comes to butchering, the old saying, "Cleanliness is next to Godliness," says it all. Keep everything clean and disinfected.

the meat. Clean all surfaces with extremely hot, soapy water with a little bleach or disinfectant added and rinse with clean, hot water.

A solution of bleach, soap, and water kept in a spray bottle can also be useful in cleaning surfaces and equipment. Always follow by rinsing with clean, hot water. Be sure to clean and sanitize all equipment before using, after using, and before storing away as well. Wear food-safe rubber gloves as needed during all wild game field dressing and gutting. Because ground meat has more surface area than whole

LEFT: Use a disinfectant after each butchering chore and again before using tools or work surfaces.

meat, it is more susceptible to bacteria. Always make sure your hands and nails are scrupulously clean and wear food-safe gloves while handling, grinding, and mixing ground meat.

Preservation

It's also important to follow food storage times and proper preservation methods to ensure safe meat. In addition to using the meat fresh, it can be dried, frozen, or pressure canned. Follow all safety measures in preparing meat for freezing as well as in canning.

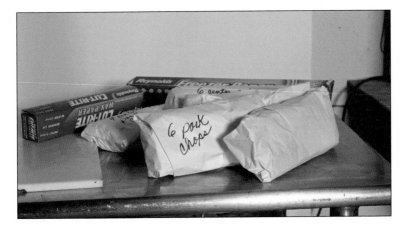

ABOVE: Package, label, and store all meat properly.

③

Poultry

FROM SUNDAY FRIED chicken dinner to the Thanksgiving turkey, poultry has traditionally been, and still is, a very important and popular meat. In the past, when folks raised their own meat, poultry was more commonly a seasonal meat, with summer broilers followed by the longer growing season needed for turkeys in the fall. Today poultry, especially chicken, is a very popular meat every day, all year long. And with good reason; poultry is good for you. Poultry provides high-quality protein, with the amino acids necessary for growth and health. Chicken and turkey also have fewer calories per serving than many other meats.

Chickens

Chickens were an important part of our family. My grandfather raised purebred chickens, selling the eggs to the many hatcheries in our area. On our farm, we had the traditional hen house for producing our own eggs. My dad also made an ingenious pull-around confinement house for raising chickens for meat. It easily raised twenty-five

ABOVE: Poultry is one of the most popular and versatile of meats. Poultry, especially chickens, are a very common farm and homestead source of meat. A wide variety of chicken breeds is available.

chickens, start to finish. A brooder arrangement in the back, with a piece of tin covered with sand and a kerosene heater underneath, it provided a warm start for day-old chicks. The front had a roof and hardware cloth sides and bottom. Lift-up trays on the sides provided a means of feeding, with waterers placed in the front. After raising a batch of chickens, we simply pulled the house to another location, providing a steady source of chicken manure for our garden. When my wife Joan and I bought our farm, we inherited my dad's confinement house. Along with our henhouse for eggs, and a good number of free-ranging birds, we raised a lot of chickens to feed a family of five.

Choosing

There are chickens and then there are *chickens*. A number of different breeds are available, actually well over fifty recognized breeds. Each of the breeds may also have different varieties, depending on plumage, coloring, and other characteristics. Some chickens are bred for laying eggs, some primarily for meat, and some are dual-purpose breeds that are more versatile and can be used for both. The egg layers, such as the leghorns, have less meat on them, as they are bred to put their energies into producing eggs. They are smaller and tend to be tougher. This is where the traditional stewing hen usually came from—at the end of a hen's productive egg-laying. The pure meat breeds are usually a cross, with Plymouth Rock and Cornish a common cross. These are typically advertised by hatcheries as meat birds. They are heavy bodied and grow fast. The dual-purpose breeds offer the opportunity for eggs or chickens for meat. A number of these traditional breeds are very popular, including:Plymouth Rock and Rhode Island Red. If purchasing day-old chicks to raise they are sold as either pullets, cockerels, or "straight run," which means the chicks haven't been sorted for sex. Straight run chicks are cheaper and you'll have both pullets for eggs and cockerels for fryers, but it's a gamble as to how many of each. One year my wife decided to "economize" when she saw a hatchery ad for an amazingly cheap batch of chicks. We ended up with an assortment of twenty-five of the skinniest, meanest exotic birds you can imagine. We had to free-range them as they fought constantly in the confinement house. They watched for

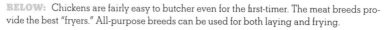

BELOW: Chickens are fairly easy to butcher even for the first-timer. The meat breeds provide the best "fryers." All-purpose breeds can be used for both laying and frying.

our youngest child, Michael, to leave the house and then took after him with a vengeance. They were so tough we could hardly eat them even stewed.

The best eating chickens are broiler-fryers, usually ready to butcher at one and a half to two pounds in eight to nine weeks, depending on the variety, feed availability, and whether raised in confinement or free-ranged. If you raise your own you can choose the variety and the method used. Confinement birds grow faster, tend to be heavier, but also have more fat content than free-range birds. There is also a somewhat subtle difference in flavor. Raising chickens to sell as butcher birds has become increasingly popular in many parts of the country, some growers selling the birds at farmers markets, others off the farm. Some will even custom butcher for you. Butchering a chicken, however, is fairly easy, and less daunting than butchering larger animals. Chickens are a great way to get started in home butchering because they don't require a lot of special tools or a big workplace.

Killing

Killing anything is hard for most of us. But it is a necessary chore for the home butcher. Our son Michael sure didn't mind the fighting roosters getting their due. It's important to butcher with the least amount of pain and suffering for the bird. Before you begin the butchering process, remove feed for twelve hours, but allow plenty of water. This helps clean out the intestines, making for easier butchering. Have everything on hand and ready to butcher, including scalding water. If you're butchering more than one or two birds, a helper is probably needed, one to kill and one to dip and pluck the birds. The quicker the birds are plucked, the easier it is to remove the feathers before they "set." Even with two working it's best to kill no more than four to six chickens at a time, then scald and pluck them.

The next step is catching the chickens and that is sometimes the hardest part. You need to keep the birds as calm as possible during this process, it's not only less stressful for you, but also provides better meat. For many years a neighbor of ours raised thousands of

ABOVE: The birds should be confined so they're easily caught with little stress just before slaughter.

chickens in their broiler houses and when it came time to ship out the broilers, neighborhood kids were hired. It was good money for a few hours of hot, hard, dusty, and unpleasant work. As the neighborhood kids became teenagers, they all worked at the job. Good catchers could catch and hold as many as six or more chickens in each hand, then carry them to the cages in the waiting transport trucks. The task took place after dark, and large nets were used to corral the birds toward the end of the long buildings. The last few birds became extremely wary and often took as much time to catch as all the rest. You'll find the same problem with catching your own chickens. Pen them as tightly as possible before catching, but the last few will become excited and harder to catch. Catch one bird at a time and carry them to the killing area head down, holding their wings to their feet to keep them from flapping their wings.

Chickens can be killed in any number of ways. The old-timers often simply grabbed the chicken by the head, gave a quick spin and twist and "wrung the neck," but this method takes skill. The traditional method used by our family for generations was the venerable chopping block. You'll need a sturdy wooden block and a sharp hand

ABOVE: The most humane method of killing chickens utilizes a killing cone, such as this plastic bucket with a hole in the bottom.

axe. A section of cut-off log about twenty-four inches long is an ideal choice for a chopping block, and the axe should have a wide head. Once you catch the chicken, hold it with the wings against the legs with one hand and head down as you carry it to the chopping block, the axe held in the opposite hand. Position the head on the chopping block and with a decisive swing, cut off the head about halfway down the neck. I know, this will usually take practice and for some a bit of grit. With the head off, we would simply toss the bird onto the grass, where it would flop for a few minutes. This "bleeding out" period is important. This method of killing is often difficult for the inexperienced.

Another traditional method is to hang the bird by its feet, then slice across the jugular vein at the base of the neck with a sharp knife. Immediately stick the sharp point of the knife through the roof of the mouth and into the brain at the back of the head. Many feel this not only humanely kills the bird, but releases the feathers so they will pluck easier. Some also prefer to first "kill" the bird by sticking the brain, then cutting the jugular vein. With any method there will be blood. Some folks also advocate the use of a "blood-cup" or discarded tin can to catch the blood.

ABOVE: The head is pulled down and slightly out to stretch the neck and the throat is cut. Once the carcass stops flopping, cut off the head.

The use of a "killing cone" makes the chore easier for some. The cone holds the bird securely for killing, prevents the bird from flopping around, which in some cases can cause bruising of the meat, and cuts down on the blood splatter. You can purchase killing cones from farm-supply and butcher-supply houses, but you can also make your own quite easily. Any plastic funnel, or jug with the neck cut down large enough to allow the bird's head to fit through will do. I use a two-gallon plastic bucket with a two-inch hole in the center of the bucket bottom. You will have to support the cone in some manner, and a 2x4 support frame can be attached to an outbuilding wall, or made freestanding. I simply tie my bucket cone to our clothesline pole.

Plucking

Removing the feathers is probably the hardest part of slaughtering chickens. Chickens can be dry plucked or scalded and then plucked. Farm wives often dry plucked the bird when slaughtering only one or two birds for immediate table use. Dry plucking is somewhat hard and time-consuming, but some say the meat is better qual-

ABOVE: Wet plucking is the most common method of removing the feathers. Water is heated in an old canner or similar pot to between 126°F and 130°F.

ity. Scalding and wet plucking is the best choice for doing more than one or two birds. At best, scalding and plucking is a messy, hot, and dirty job. You'll need a fire and a pot large enough to immerse the entire chicken. In the past I simply built a campfire-style wood fire with a pair of concrete blocks on either side to support an old canning kettle.

It's often difficult to keep this type of fire regulated and you need a water temperature of around 126°F to 130°F. Hotter and the skin may tear when you try to pull out the feathers, and you also run the risk of damaging the outer yellow, cuticle layer of skin. If the water is too cool, the feathers may not release. I've discovered a turkey-fryer, or fish-fryer burner works best.

With a thermometer in the water you can keep the water tempera-ture regulated more easily. You can also heat water to the boiling point on your kitchen stove, and pour it into the kettle or pot. Whatever pot you use should be relegated primarily to this chore, as it really gets nasty and hard to clean. Dip the entire bird down into the scald-ing water, dunk it up and down several times and swish it around to make sure the scalding water gets in and around all the feathers. Be

ABOVE: Dunk the carcass in the hot water, then swirl around several times. Immerse for about thirty seconds total.

careful not to splash scalding water on yourself or any helpers. The time should be around thirty seconds. Younger birds will take less time than older birds. For older birds this may need to be a minute

BELOW: Lay the bird on a newspaper and immediately begin plucking. Start with the wings and tail feathers.

ABOVE: Work quickly to pluck out all the feathers.

or longer. Test to see if the wing or tail feathers come out easily, if not dip again.

Hang the bird, or lay it on a table and begin plucking. Start with the wing feathers and work as fast as you can. As the skin cools, it becomes harder to pluck the feathers.

Then work on the breast feathers, followed by the sides and back. Pluck the leg feathers last. If some feathers don't remove easily, dip again.

If only the legs need dipping, hold the chicken by the wings to dip the legs. If dipping a number of chickens, you will probably need

BELOW: Make sure to get to all areas of the bird, such as under the wings.

BELOW: Pull out and scrape off any pin feathers.

ABOVE: Using a propane torch, singe off any hairs.

to change the water several times, as it becomes quite nasty. You also lose some water with each dipping.

A number of pin feathers will be left after the main feathers are removed. These can be fairly easy, or tough, to remove, depending on the age and breed of the bird. On young meat birds the chore is fairly easy; on older and egg-layer or exotic birds, it can be tougher. Remove the pin feathers by pinching them between a paring knife blade and your thumb, or you can use tweezers. Some birds may also have hair.

Singe this off with a propane torch. You can use a gas stove burner, but remember burning hair stinks. Once all feathers have been removed, wash the carcass thoroughly in cold, running water. Old-timers often had a summer kitchen, complete with stove.

Not only did this keep the heat out of the house for summer cooking and canning, but also the smell for those who did a lot of chicken slaughtering.

Eviscerating

Chickens should be eviscerated as soon as they are plucked. The sooner you can do this chore and chill the carcass down to 40°F, the safer and better the meat. Wear food-safe gloves for this chore if you

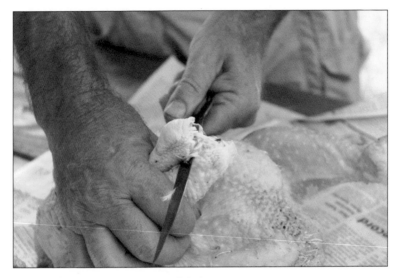

ABOVE: Bend the legs back and cut off the feet.

have any cuts or open wounds on your hands or if you are more comfortable wearing gloves.

If you haven't already removed the head, cut it off. Cut off the feet at the hock joint. Bend the joint to find the tendons and cut through them. In some cultures, the feet are considered a delicacy.

BELOW: Cut off the neck and remove the neck skin, crop, gullet, and windpipe.

ABOVE: To eviscerate for whole, or traditional, cut-up frying chicken, make a cut from the breastbone to the vent, being extremely careful not to cut into the intestines and the anus.

ABOVE: Continue the cut to encircle the anus.

Lay the bird on its back, with the belly facing you. Pinch up the belly skin, insert a small, sharp, rounded-tip knife blade just under the breastbone (or keel), blade edge up, and cut to the vent, being careful not to cut into the intestines. It's important to prevent feces from getting on the meat. One of two methods can be used. The first is to continue the cut made from the breastbone to encircle the anus.

In this case you must reach inside the body cavity and use your fingers to move the intestine around to keep from cutting into it.

BELOW: Reach in and pull out the intestines, including gizzard, heart, and lungs. Cut off crop and gullet.

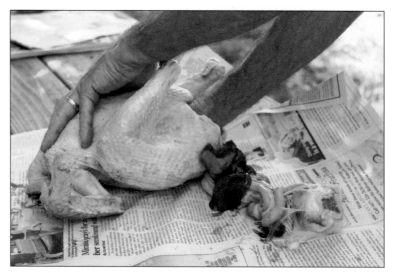

Then reach into the body cavity and pull out the intestines along with the anus. It will usually take a bit of effort in order to remove the crop and windpipe. Be careful not to tear the intestines.

In most instances, you'll have to reach back in and remove the gizzard, heart, and lungs. Use your fingers to scrape away the gonads on the underside of the backbone. Cut off the neck and remove the crop, gullet, and neck skin.

Another method I use is to first make a cut at the shoulder point then around the back of the neck and remove the neck skin, crop, gullet and windpipe. I cut off the neck at the shoulder joint, twisting the neck as needed to cut through the muscle and bone. Then I make the belly cut, and pull out the intestines. As I reach the anus, I cut around it to release everything. There is less chance of cutting into the intestines using this method.

Cut away the oil gland on the back, near the top of the tail. Wash the interior of the carcass with cold, running water and immediately place into ice water. Some folks like to add about a cup of salt to the ice water. Carefully cut the gallbladder from the liver. Do not cut into the bladder or bile sac on the liver because the nasty green bile will ruin the taste of any meat it touches. Trim off the end of the heart. Using

BELOW: Carefully cut away the oil gland on the upper back of the tail.

LEFT: Immediately place the carcass in ice water to chill before cutting up.

RIGHT: Remove the heart and liver from the viscera, then very carefully cut away the gall bladder from the liver.

LEFT: Split the gizzard with a sharp knife, making the cut on the gizzard's opening side.

LEFT: Pull the split gizzard apart.

RIGHT: Peel out the inner membrane.

LEFT: The cleaned gizzard.

a sharp knife, slice around the outside edge of the gizzard. Peel away the inner lining and wash the gizzard thoroughly. Wash the heart, liver, and gizzard in cold, running water and place all in a pan of ice water to chill.

Discard the offal and feathers in your compost heap, making sure they are well covered with soil. Or you may wish to bury them.

Cutting Up

Depending on how the chicken is to be cooked and served, you may leave the carcass whole, or cut it into serving pieces. For a stewing hen, or to smoke in a smoker, the carcass is usually left whole. To freeze, the bird is usually left whole. To barbeque, the carcass is often split to produce chicken "halves." For frying, the carcass is cut into smaller pieces in order to properly fry.

Splitting a broiler/fryer is fairly easy to do, and in fact, you can incorporate the splitting and eviscerating into one operation. After plucking, remove the feet, cut off the oil gland, and cut off the neck close to the body. Using a pair of sturdy kitchen shears, start at the neck and split the backbone down to the anus. This is fairly easy on a

BELOW: Chicken carcasses can be left whole or split in half for broiling, grilling, and other recipes.

RIGHT: In this case, the carcass is eviscerated at the same time it is split. Cut down the backbone with shears, separating the two halves.

LEFT: The entire intestines can then easily be pulled out of the carcass.

RIGHT: On older birds cut on both sides of the backbone.

LEFT: You can use kitchen shears or a knife to cut out the backbone.

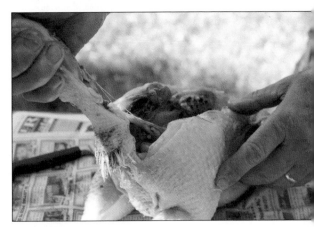

RIGHT: Then pull out the backbone with the intestines.

LEFT: Wash the carcass thoroughly in cold, running water and chill in ice water.

young broiler. On older birds, leave the neck in place and cut on each side of the backbone. You can also stand the bird on its rear end and use a sharp, short knife for the chore, but the shears are safest. In either case, spread open the bird. On split backbones, use a knife to cut around the vent. Grasp the organs and pull them out. On a separated backbone, cut around the esophagus and vent, then remove the backbone and intestines, cutting the tissues free. The backbone and included neck can be kept for soup stock or broth. Using the shears, cut through the V of the wishbone, then cut down the center of the breastbone to separate the carcass into two halves. You can also continue cutting up the carcass into smaller pieces for frying.

When preparing a chicken for frying, however, in most instances the bird will be plucked, eviscerated, and cut up into the classic eight, ten, or twelve pieces. Cutting the bird into smaller pieces that are fairly even in size makes it easier to fry properly. For fresh fried chicken cut up the bird immediately after proper chilling. If you plan to freeze the bird, however, the best tactic is to freeze the whole carcass, then thaw properly, and cut up into frying pieces just before frying. Smaller pieces tend to freezer burn and dry out more rapidly than the whole chicken.

BELOW: Chicken carcasses can be left whole or cut up in several ways for frying, creating eight, ten, or twelve pieces.

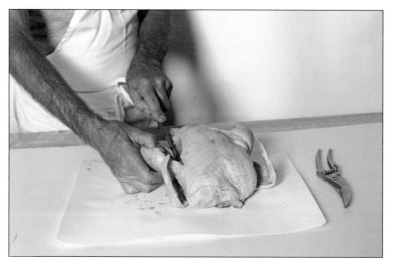

Classic Eight-Piece (two drumsticks, two thighs, two wings, two breast halves)

Position the bird on its back on a cutting board, with the legs facing you. Cut through the skin down between the thighs and the body. Holding the body, push down a leg until you hear it snap and disjoint. Then cut around and through the joint, avoiding cutting into the bone. Bend the leg and thigh together to locate the knee joint, and cut

ABOVE: The first step is to remove the legs and thighs. Pull the leg away from the body and cut through the skin and muscle between the two.

BELOW: Continue pulling and cutting until you can "pop" the joint.

through it. Again, avoid cutting through the bones. This may take a bit of practice. Repeat the step for the opposite leg. Remove a wing by stretching it out to the side, then cutting between the wing bone and the body. Remove the small wing tip and use for soup stock. Stand the chicken on its rear end and cut between the backbone and ribs and the rest of the chicken. Make the cut on the opposite side. The backbone can be used for soup stock as well. Lay the breast on the cutting board and cut down through the center.

ABOVE: Cut through the remainder of the skin and muscle.

BELOW: Bend the leg and thigh to find the joint and make a starting cut.

LEFT: Lay the leg and thigh down on the cutting board and continue the cut to separate the two.

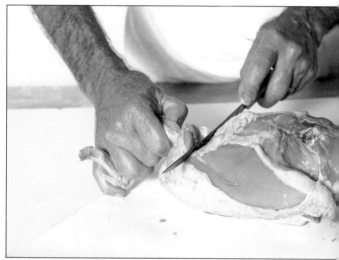

RIGHT: Pull back the wing and separate it from the carcass.

LEFT: Cut off the wing tip if desired and save for the soup pot.

RIGHT: Split the breastbone.

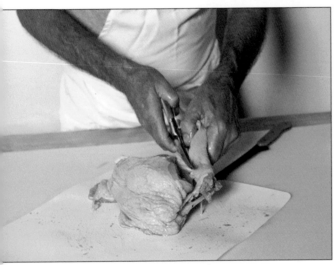

LEFT: Split or remove the backbone.

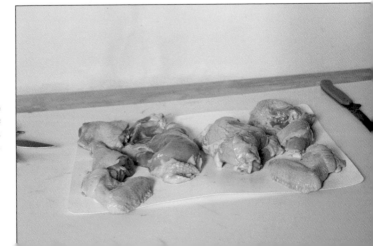

RIGHT: The resulting classic eight-piece chicken for frying.

Ten-Piece (two drumsticks, two thighs, two wings, four breast pieces)

To create, cut the classic eight-piece and then cut the two breast pieces in half crosswise.

ABOVE: To create ten pieces, cut the breast pieces in half.

BELOW: Ten-piece cut.

Twelve-Piece (two drumsticks, two thighs, two winglets, two drumettes, four breast pieces)

Again, cut the classic eight-piece, then cut the breast into four pieces and the wings into drumettes and winglets, cutting at the joint.

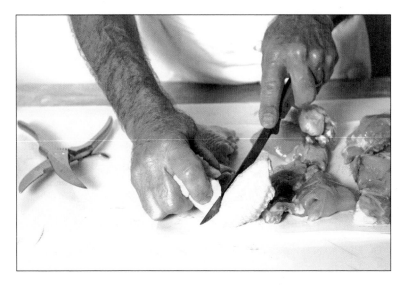

ABOVE: To create twelve pieces, cut the wings into winglets and drumettes.

BELOW: The resulting twelve-piece cuts.

Boned-Out Chicken

Our family has used a different method to again create even-sized frying pieces, as well as better utilize the entire chicken. The wings are removed and cut into winglets and drumettes, and legs and thighs are removed and cut into individual legs and thighs. The thighs are then boned out. This is a fairly easy chore. Make a cut on the inside of the thigh and then cut around the bone with a sharp boning knife. The breast is also boned out by cutting down the keel bone with a sharp boning knife, then following the rib cage to cut away the breast meat. Each of the breast halves is then cut into two pieces. This method is quite simple, and leaves the neck intact with the rib cage. The boned-out carcass, wing tips, and thigh bones are placed in

BELOW: Another method utilizes partially boned-out pieces. Remove the legs, thighs, and wings.

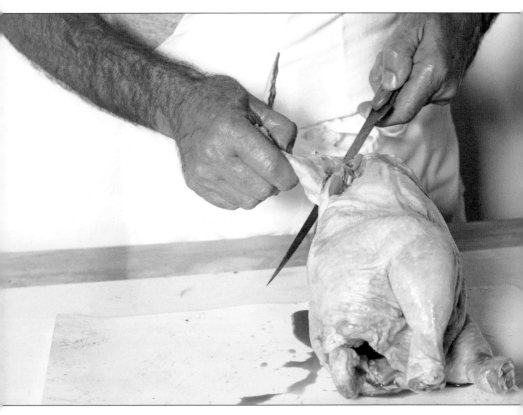

ABOVE: Separate the legs and thighs. Use a sharp boning knife to bone out the thighs.

BELOW: Save the thigh bones for the soup pot.

ABOVE: Bone out the breast by cutting to one side of the breastbone.

BELOW: Continue cutting around the ribcage and pull the breast meat away.

ABOVE: Cut each breast piece in half.

BELOW: Save the boned-out carcass for the soup pot.

a large pot with water and salt, along with onion, carrots, and celery if desired. The bones are simmered until thoroughly cooked, allowed to cool, then the meat is picked off the bones. The broth is strained, placed in a refrigerator and allowed to cool, and the fat is skimmed off the broth. The broth and meat are frozen, either individually or together for use in soups, noodles, and other dishes. This soup stock/broth could also be pressure canned.

Turkeys

Turkeys are killed, eviscerated, and plucked in basically the same manner as chickens. It is a bigger, harder job, but you can butcher your own Thanksgiving or Christmas turkey. Most who do this will have raised the birds as well. If purchasing turkeys to butcher, it's important to know their age. Purchased turkeys may be young or old, and it's hard to tell the age of a mature bird. Yearling turkeys are the best choice, as the old birds can really be tough, especially if they're grass raised. Turkeys are hard to catch, hold, and kill. They can flog and spur, inflicting considerable damage. The best tactic is to slowly and gently crowd them into a very tiny enclosure. When you grasp their feet, at the same time wrap your arm around their body to hold the wings in tight. It can still be a battle. Some prefer to stun the birds with a blow to the back of the skull with a large club. The traditional Thanksgiving cartoons show the turkey and a chopping block, but the best method of killing a turkey is to use a killing cone. You can make one quite easily by cutting a five-inch-diameter hole in the bottom of a five-gallon plastic bucket. Insert the bird's head into the hole and immediately cut its throat. Turkeys are also a bit harder to pluck. You will, of course, need a larger pot of scalding water and the water temperature should be increased slightly to around 130°F. Turkeys are usually eviscerated and left whole. The neck is skinned out and the neck and crop are removed. The neck skin is then used to seal around the opening during roasting.

ABOVE: Turkeys are butchered in much the same manner as chickens except they're normally left whole.

Ducks

Again, the age of the bird is important. If you've raised your own fowl, no problem, but be sure to ask the age of purchased ready-to-butcher ducks. Commercially available ducks are labeled as duckling, young duckling, broiler duckling, fryer duckling, or roaster duckling, depending on the age. Ducks are normally killed and eviscerated the same way as for whole chickens. Some like to "hang" the eviscerated ducks for a few days to age. Any aging should be done in a temperature between 35°F and 45°F. Ducks may be dry plucked, wet plucked, or wax plucked. Some like to merely skin the birds if they are to be used in gumbo, ground into sausages, or for other dishes. Simply split the skin along the breastbone and peel off the skin to either side. However, take care when skinning the breast and back because the skin there is fairly hard to remove. Skin, remove legs, feet, and head, and eviscerate.

Dry Plucking

Dry plucking provides the best appearance, but is harder to do and takes more time. Simply pluck the feathers, holding the bird over a paper sack to catch the feathers and down. Start at the top of the breast and dry pluck downward. Plucking the feathers in the same direction that they lay prevents tearing them out and damaging the skin. After plucking the breast, do the sides, then the back. The back is the hardest to do, and sometimes takes a bit of effort to remove the feathers. Cutting off the wing tips helps keep them out of the way and makes for easier plucking. Use a hand torch to singe

BELOW: Ducks and geese are often dry plucked.

off the hairs. If you do any amount of dry plucking on ducks, geese or other poultry, you may wish to invest in a mechanical plucker. It has a rotating drum with rubber fingers to quickly and easily remove feathers.

Wet Plucking

Wet plucking is easier to do, especially if you have several ducks. Ducks can be wet plucked with scalding water, to which you've added a bit of dishwashing detergent to help soak into the feathers. The temperature should be higher, around 140°F. As with chickens, the birds are plucked, then eviscerated.

Wax Plucking

Wax plucking is the easiest method, but the birds should not first be eviscerated. Paraffin wax is melted in a double boiler arrangement. Place a pot or pan large enough for dipping the ducks in a larger

BELOW: Or they are first dunked in melted wax, and the feathers and wax pulled off.

container filled with water. Wax is highly flammable and this prevents the wax from catching on fire. Caution: do not allow the flames to contact the wax or the wax container. You'll need about five pounds of wax. Heat the wax until it turns liquid, but do not allow it to boil. As you wait for the wax to heat up, clip off the wing tips. This allows you to more easily coat the entire carcass with wax. Some like to cut off the entire wings. If the duck head is still in place, after using a killing cone, remove the feet. Use the head to hold the duck and while dipping, force more wax into and around the feathers. Dip the bird into the wax and use an old wooden spoon or a stick to push the carcass down into the wax. Do not get any hot wax on you. Once the bird has been dipped thoroughly, remove and place on a newspaper for the wax to cool. If you have several ducks, dip them all, and place them on newspapers to cool. It's a good idea to allow the wax on the birds to cool, and then dip again to ensure you have a good solid wax coating over the entire bird. Once the ducks have acquired a good solid coating and the wax has hardened, which takes only a few minutes, grasp a handful of feathers and wax and pull off. Continue plucking until you have the feathers removed. In some instances, you may have to dip again to get all the inner layers of down removed. Singe small feathers and hairs with a propane torch.

Eviscerate as quickly as possible after plucking. Pinch up the belly skin and muscle and slice across, but not into the entrails. Pull the tip of the breastbone back and reach in and remove the entrails, pulling them downward toward the tail. Cut off the tail and vent with the entrails attached. Or, you can cut down on either side of the backbone to create a split bird, removing the entrails after cutting the backbone and neck free. If the bird is a wild, hunted duck, remove any shot and cut away any bloody areas.

Place the globs of wax and feathers in an old pot, and reheat until the wax again liquefies. Skim off the larger feathers with an old kitchen skimmer. Keep the wax in the pot for another use. As you can guess, you'll want to use an old recycled pot as it will be almost impossible to clean.

Geese

If you think ducks are hard to kill and pluck, geese are even harder. A big gander is hard to handle. Again, stunning with a blow to the back of the head is often the best choice, followed by cutting its throat in a killing cone. Geese are more popular in other countries than in the United States, where they are sometimes marketed as "green" geese at ten to thirteen weeks of age, or more commonly at six months of age. Geese are usually dry plucked, as much to save the down as to present a good carcass appearance. An automatic plucking machine is great for this chore. Geese can be hot-water plucked, but the temperature should be higher, around 150°F to 160°F. Regardless, you'll have lots of pin feathers to remove and hair and small sections of down to singe.

Storage

Regardless of the poultry being processed, all must be washed thoroughly in cold, running water, and then chilled as quickly as possible down to 40°F. The best method is in a tub of ice water. Once chilled, remove the birds from the ice-water bath and drain for about ten minutes. Place the gizzards, liver, and heart in small sections of plastic food wrap or a small plastic bag and insert into the carcass. Place the carcass in a plastic food bag. Properly chilled poultry can be stored in the coldest part of the refrigerator for up to two days before they are consumed. If freezing, the birds should be frozen immediately. Place in plastic food bags, extract as much air as possible and tie tightly shut. Double wrapping helps extend the storage time. The use of a vacuum packer can also increase storage times. Do not place a large quantity of unfrozen items in your freezer at the same time. This can put too much of a load on the freezer, with slow freezing and possibly partial thawing.

④

Hog Butchering

GROWING UP ON a central Missouri farm in the '40s and '50s, I remember hog butchering days as a celebration. The annual winter event took place at my granddad's, with several uncles, aunts, cousins, and neighbors joining in. The group often butchered a dozen or more hogs. Everyone worked together. Each of the men and women had a specific job, with several specialists, such as my granddad, in curing the hams. There was lots of fun, laughter, and great food, and we knew everyone had meat for the winter.

These days most of us don't participate in that type of "butchering days," but you can still butcher your own hog. Some of the old methods are used today, but newer methods have developed as well. You will probably need some special equipment, as described in Chapter One. Butchering a pig takes work—you can plan on at least two days for the initial butchering and a third day to finish up. The first day consists of the killing and dressing the hog. The carcass is allowed to cool overnight, and is cut up the second day. The third day usually consists of making such things as headcheese, sausage, and rendering the lard. With a big group working together, this was usually accomplished in two days, even with a number of hogs, but if you're doing it by yourself or with a friend or two, you'd better set aside three

ABOVE: Pork is a traditional meat in many countries, providing a wide variety of meats, including fresh meats, salted and cured meats, and ground sausage. The author and brother with a pair of prizewinning pigs.

days. It also takes quite a bit of getting ready to butcher a hog, so you might as well figure on the day before for that chore.

Choosing

Hogs are definitely different than they were a century ago. Back in those days a "fat hog," ready to butcher, was just that—fat, often weighing 300 to 350 pounds. Photos of hogs from that period looked like a barrel with almost no legs, their bellies touching the ground. Today's hogs have been bred to be extremely lean, with a lot less body fat, long legs, and a long-framed body. While still in grade school, I entered a contest sponsored by the Sears Foundation and won a registered, bred Duroc gilt. The rules stated I had to give a gilt from my pig's first litter back to the foundation, which I did, and I also gave one to my brother. That started me on an early hog-raising business venture. Our family showed and sold registered Duroc hogs for a number of years.

Today's pork tenderloin is just as lean as skinless chicken breast, with 2.98 grams of fat per a three-ounce serving and meets government guidelines for "extra lean," the reason pork is now called "the other white meat." Quality pork should have a pinkish gray color and

BELOW: Today's pork is a far cry from the traditional "fat hogs" of yesteryear. Today's pork is a leaner and healthier meat.

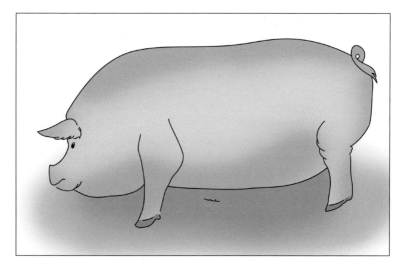

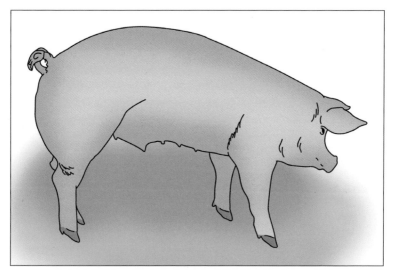

be quite lean, with streaks of firm white fat. The meat should be fine in texture and the outer layer of fat should be creamy white and not too thick. Whether you butcher your own, or purchase a pig ready to butcher, the ideal weight is 180 to 200 pounds live weight, and at five to six months in age.

Killing

Some experts suggest keeping feed from the animal for twenty-four hours before slaughter. I prefer to feed mid-afternoon the day before butchering, and keep feed away the evening before. A handful of feed at killing time makes it easier to confine and kill the animal. Water, however, should not be withheld. Killing the animal should be as quick and painless as possible, not only for the animal's sake, but also for the quality of the meat. Make every effort to keep the animal from getting excited or scared. When an animal becomes scared, the adrenalin goes up and lactic acid is released into the system.

BELOW: Home-butchered hogs are usually killed by first stunning with a .22 bullet.

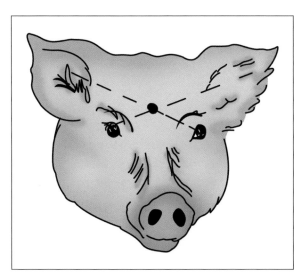

Blood also flushes throughout the system. "Makes the meat 'fiery,'" my granddad used to say, "And the hams and sides won't cure properly." Several years ago I experienced the problem. An older neighbor asked me to help butcher a hog. His eyesight wasn't so good and when he shot the pig to stun it, he missed his mark and shot the unfortunate hog in the snout. The enraged pig busted out of the pen and started running. After a pickup chase and several shots, he finally killed the pig. The pig didn't bleed out properly when stuck. When we dressed the animal and even the day after when cutting up the meat, blood still oozed from all portions of the meat. I never got a taste, but my neighbor said the meat "wasn't fit to eat," and I then knew what Granddad meant.

The most common method of killing a hog is with a .22 bullet to the brain, stunning the animal, then immediately "sticking" to bleed out. Confine the animal to a chute, small pen, or even a killing crate. The latter has a drop-down side making it easy to get to the downed pig. Place some food to get the pig's attention, and make the shot with the gun barrel as close to the skull as you can to ensure a good hit. The shot should be in the middle of the forehead and just above and between the eyes. The barrel of the gun must be at a right angle to the line of the snout and forehead, otherwise the slug may be above or below the center of the brain area and into the sinuses or above the main brain area. If you're standing to make the shot, you can easily shoot too low. Make the shot from a low angle. Shot properly, the stunned pig will drop to the ground immediately. It may lie still, or begin kicking spastically. The hog must then be "stuck" in order to bleed out properly. Be very careful with this chore, as a sharp knife and a kicking hog can be dangerous. You can easily be injured by an animal's kicking legs. A guide I knew in Idaho died on a mountainside when he was field dressing an elk and the animal's kick cut his femoral artery.

Sticking must be done immediately and may be done in one of two ways. The most common method is on the ground. A helper can be a great assist, although a strong person can do this alone. Grasp a front leg and roll the pig onto its back, straddling the pig, and again

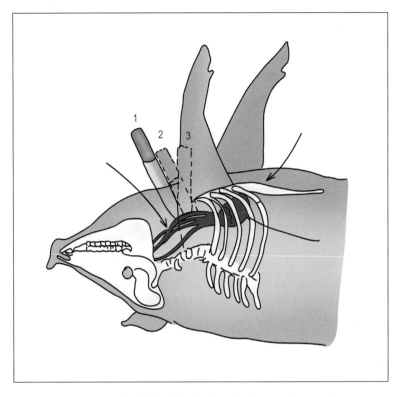

ABOVE: They are immediately "stuck" with a sharp knife to sever the carotid artery.

be careful of the kicking back feet. Or you can loop a rope around a back leg between the dewclaws and hock and hoist the pig for sticking. The idea in properly sticking is to sever the carotid artery, without damaging the surrounding meat. Simply cutting the pig's throat from ear to ear is definitely not the way to do it. You won't get a proper bleed out and the surrounding meat of the jowls and shoulders may be damaged. The artery lies in the throat and just below the breastbone point. The drawing shows the location and proper method of sticking. Any fairly long, wide-blade butcher knife will do, but the old-timers used a "sticking" knife which is sharpened on both sides of the blade. The knifepoint is inserted into the center of the throat and just forward of the point of the breastbone, with the point angled toward the rear of the animal. Push in the blade until it reaches the backbone, then swivel the blade until it is perpendicular to the throat and cut back toward the chin. The finished cut should be centered in the throat and about four inches long. Blood should gush forth in pulses. Lay the pig back down on its side to bleed out. If the blood doesn't gush forth, make the cut deeper extending more into the chest, but do not cut deep enough to get into the heart as that will interfere with proper bleeding. Lay the pig back down on its side to bleed out, or better yet, hoist the pig by the rear legs to allow for a better bleed out. Some cultures catch the blood for use in blood dishes. If keeping the blood, place a large pot under the pig and stir the blood to keep it from clotting as it collects. Hose off the hoisted pig with running water, or use buckets of water to slosh off any dirt and blood.

Scalding or Skinning

The carcass may either be scalded and scraped or skinned. The old-time, traditional method is scalding and scraping. This is the hardest method, especially if doing the chore yourself. Two people, however, can scrape a hog fairly quickly and easily. The carcass of a scraped hog has a better appearance, you have the skin on for ham protection, and there is more fat for lard. The most common method these days, however, and especially with most slaughterhouses, is skinning.

Scalding and Scraping

If scalding, the water must be hot and ready for use immediately after the hog is killed. This is why help can be invaluable. Someone can be in charge of the scalding water, while others attend to the killing. And you'll need help in lifting and scraping the carcass. The average-sized butcher hog can be scalded in a fifty-gallon metal barrel. You'll need to build a fire around the barrel. One method is to place the barrel on bricks or concrete blocks and build the fire in and around the bottom of the barrel. You'll also need a table near the barrel for scraping. You can use a tractor bucket or rope-and-pulley hoist for dunking and scraping, scraping the pig while hanging. Our family, however, made a sturdy table just for this purpose, about 2.5 feet high and with a notch cut in one end. The metal barrel is positioned at an angle, its top leaning into the notch. The fire is built around the bottom of the tilted barrel. The hog is lifted onto the table, then slid into the hot water to dunk, then pulled up and out onto the table to scrape. You'll need some bell scrapers, or large-bladed butcher knives. If using knives, they shouldn't be extra sharp.

The scalding water should be between 150°F and 160°F, and it may take some time to get the water hot enough. Figure on an hour or so, depending on the wood used to heat the water as well as the ambient air temperature. The water, however, should not be allowed to get hotter than 170°F, or the hair will set, the follicles shrinking and holding the bristles firmly in place. My granddad could tell if the temperature was correct by quickly dipping his fingers in the hot water. I prefer to use a kitchen thermometer to determine the water temperature. Stir

BELOW: Water is heated to between 150°F and 160°F and the hog dipped into the scalding water. You will need a large metal barrel and a sturdy table for the job.

the water before reading the temperature. If too hot, add some ice, if too cool, allow to heat more.

Once the proper temperature has been reached, dunk the pig into the hot water. In a fifty-gallon barrel, you'll only be able to dunk half a pig at a time. We basically stood on the table and two people used hay hooks through the hind-leg tendon cuts to dunk the front half. If you don't have hay hooks, each person can simply hold onto a leg each for the dipping. If you don't have the table arrangement, you can use a tractor bucket or other hoist to lower the pig into the hot water. Allow the pig to soak in the hot water for thirty to forty-five seconds, dunking it up and down several times to make sure the hot water evenly coats the carcass.

Then hoist out the pig and test it by pulling on some bristles. If the bristles come out easily, the carcass is ready to scrape. If not, repeat the dunking only for a shorter time. Scraping on a table is the easiest, although you can also scrape the hog while it's hanging. Lay

BELOW: A knife or bell scraper is then used to scrape off the hairs and bristles.

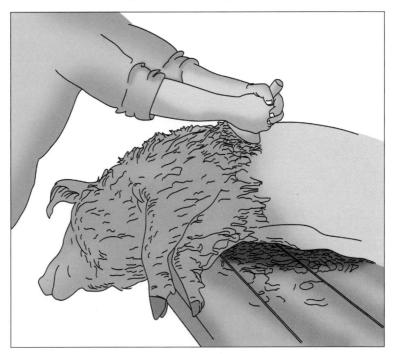

the hog down and begin with the feet and head. These not only cool down and dry quicker, but are the hardest to scrape. If you're going to save the feet for pickled pigs' feet, immediately pull off the dewclaws with a pair of pliers. Work from the head and feet toward the sides and back. If the hide begins to dry, douse it with a bucket of hot water from the dipping tank. Regardless, it's important to work as quickly as possible. Knives can be used for scraping, but they should not be very sharp because it's easy to cut yourself or your buddy. It's also easy to nick and cut the carcass skin as well. Bell scrapers are the best choice. They make scraping faster, easier, and safer. It's impor- tant to remove not only the bristles, but also the scurf on the skin as well. This is hot, dirty work at best. A stiff wire brush can be used to get at bristles in the cracks and crevices of the skin around the face and feet.

Once you have the front half done, turn the pig and dip the back half in the same manner, first ensuring the water is of the correct temperature. Remember, it's best to have friends helping: one can be tending the fire while another helps scrape. Again, we used a hay hook for the dunking chore. It is driven through the mouth from the inside and under the tongue. Or, you can cut holes behind the tendons in the front legs and use a gambrel. I've seen some simply hold the pig by the front legs. This is somewhat iffy, however, as the scraped front half tends to be slippery, and if you lose the pig in the barrel of hot water, you've got problems. In any case, the dunking and scraping is done in the same manner. Scraping the back half, however, is easier than the front half. It's a good idea to keep coarse rags such as burlap on hand to wipe down and clean off the scraped hair and bristles. Once the carcass is scraped, you may wish to douse the hog with hot water and wipe down. Now you're ready to gut the carcass.

Skinning

Skinning doesn't require as much in the way of tools and equip- ment, nor will you need to build a fire and heat water. In some ways, it's also less messy to skin. Although hogs can be partially skinned

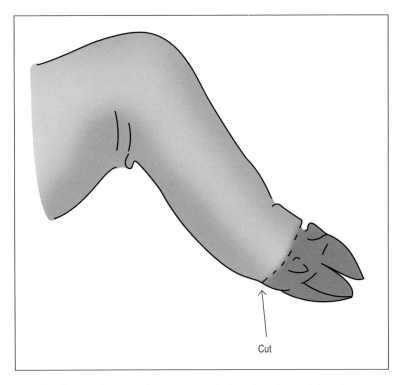

Cut

ABOVE: Skinning the carcass is more commonly done these days and doesn't require as much skill or tools. The first step is to cut off the feet.

lying on the ground, I prefer to hang the hog head down for all skinning. You can gut the hog first and then skin, or skin and then gut, my preferred method.

The first step in skinning is to cut off the feet at the knee joints in front and about three inches below the hocks on the back, leaving plenty of heel tendons. Then cut between the tendons and the legs to insert a gambrel. Hoist the pig off the ground, and make a cut from the rear of the pig down the belly to the jaw tip. Make sure you don't cut through the abdominal wall on the belly.

A gut-hook knife is great for this, or use a rounded-tip skinning knife with the blade held low to the skin to prevent cutting into the belly. Make a cut on the inside of the forelegs from the cut-off joint to the centerline cut. Then make a similar cut on the inside of each hind leg.

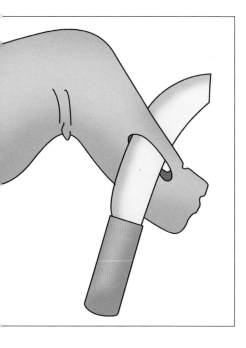

LEFT: Make a cut between the tendons and legs, insert a gambrel, and hoist the carcass on a sturdy meat pole.

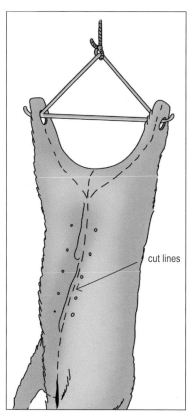

cut lines

RIGHT: Make a cut from the rear of the animal down to the jaw, making sure you don't cut through the abdominal muscles. A gut-hook knife works well for this. Then make a cut on the inside of each leg. Cut away the pizzle if it's a male hog.

Hog hide is thick and tough and the fat adheres to it. Skinning the whole hide, in the manner of a deer or beef, is impossible. The best method is to make shallow cuts through the skin about two to three inches apart, starting at the rear or hams and down the sides and back to the head. The inside of the legs and belly skin is thinner and it's not necessary to strip cut these areas. A sharp vinyl flooring, carpet, or even a hooked roofing knife makes the chore easy, as long as the blade tip is sharp. Try to keep from cutting deeper than just below the skin. Once the strip cuts are made, I prefer to start skinning at the front

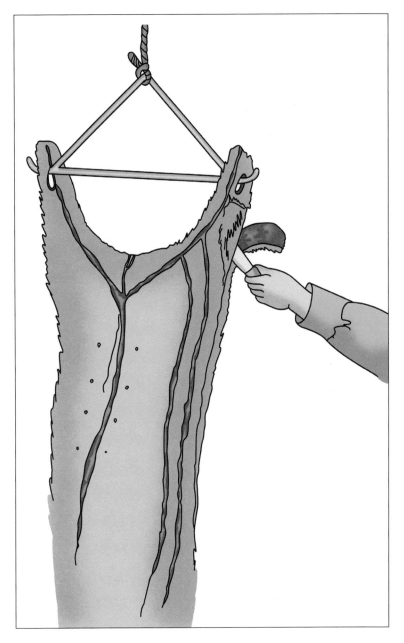

ABOVE: Hog skin is thick and tough. Slitting the skin with a sharp hooked knife into strips two to three inches wide makes the chore easier.

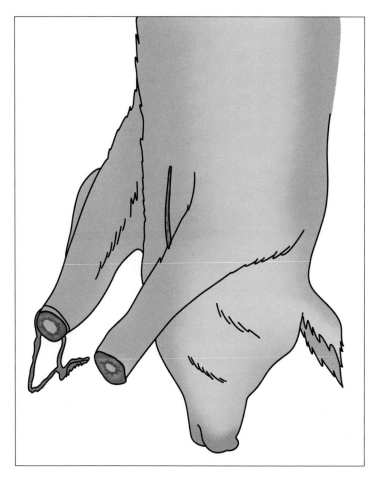

ABOVE: Skin out the front legs first.

legs. As the skin is removed from the rear and hangs down over the front it makes skinning the forelegs harder.

Start skinning by using a skinning knife to slide under the skin at the leg cut line where the feet have been cut off. Hold the skin with one hand and continue to slice the skin away from the carcass.

ABOVE: Beginning at the inside of the rear legs, skin back over the hams. Continue skinning down the sides and back to the head.

Continue around the sides of the forelegs and also cut the skin away from the jowls.

Starting on the inside of a rear leg, make the same cut. Slice and pull the skin down around the rear leg and over the ham. This is

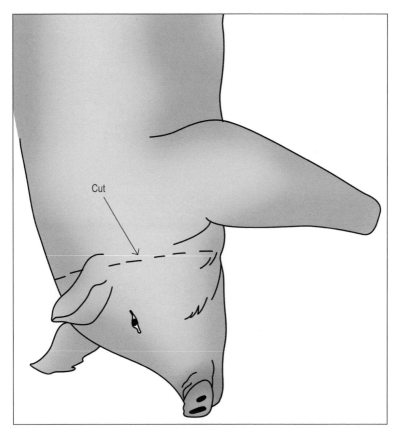

Cut

ABOVE: Cut off the head, making a cut just behind the ears and at right angles to the backbone, and then continuing around the sides and jowls. Cut to the bone and twist off the head. The head is easier skinned lying on a table.

actually the hardest part of the hog to skin, but strip cuts make the chore easier.

Skin out around the anus and penis, leaving these areas intact with the carcass. Repeat the process on the opposite leg. Skin the belly back to each side. Skin the back and sides, pulling the hide off in strips down to the head. At this point, I like to cut off the skinned-out hide, cut off the head, and then later skin out the head separately up on a table.

Gutting

Again, you can gut the carcass before skinning, however, the more common tactic is gutting after skinning. Some like to lower the pig back to the ground onto a clean tarp for the initial skinning. In the past, with a lot of help, we scalded and scraped our hogs, but I've ended up doing the job mostly by myself in later years and prefer to skin the hog. It's extremely important to gut the animal without cutting into the intestines and spilling fecal matter on the meat. If you do, make sure you thoroughly wash any matter away with lots of running water. The first step is to make a shallow cut from the jaw to the bung down the centerline of the belly. Keep the blade flat to the skin. Or best, use a gut-hook blade on a skinning knife. Do not cut through the abdominal muscle at this time. If a boar, cut away the pizzle, or penis. It lies just under the skin down the belly and runs to just below the anus. Starting at the tip, slice around and under the

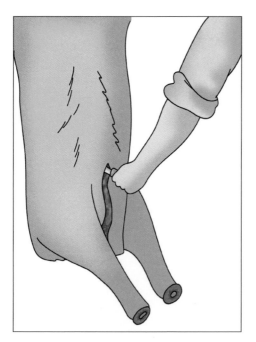

LEFT: Open the chest using a knife starting at the tip of the breastbone and cutting through the rib cage. A meat saw is often necessary.

pizzle, peeling it back as you go. When you reach where the pizzle goes into the abdomen near the anus, simply lay it back over the rear of the carcass. The next step is to open the chest. Find the back tip of the backbone and, holding a knife flat to the carcass, cut through the centerline of the muscle over the breastbone. A sturdy, sharp knife can then be used to cut through the bone and muscle following this line. Hold the knife handle up and the tip down, to ensure you don't cut into the intestines pressing against the top of the breastbone. Do not cut up past the end of the breastbone or the intestines will begin to fall out and down. Cut down to the underside of the tip of the jaw. A meat saw may be necessary for cutting through the breastbone on older animals.

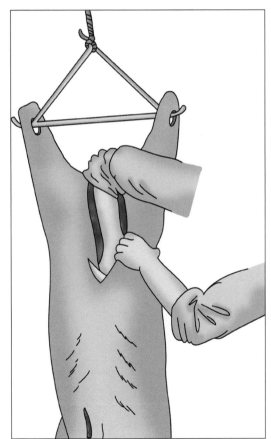

RIGHT: Using a knife cut directly between the hams down to the pelvic bone, then cut through the pelvic bone. Use a meat saw if necessary. Open the belly by positioning a knife point out and blade edge down. Make a shallow starting cut, and then insert your fist holding the knife into the abdominal cavity and push the knife downward, being careful not to cut into the intestines.

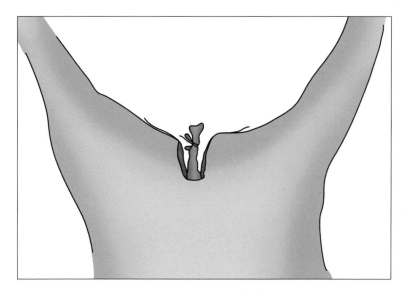

ABOVE: Go back up to the rear of the animal and cut around the bung. You may wish to tie a string around it to prevent fecal matter from contaminating the carcass.

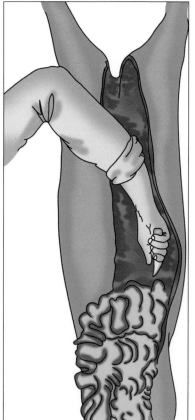

RIGHT: As the intestines fall free, cut around the diaphragm to free them and gently pull them through the chest opening. Cut off the gullet or remove the head, if it hasn't already been removed.

Now go to the opposite end of the hog and make a cut directly between the hams. If you make the cut properly, when the hams begin to separate, you'll see a white line dividing the hams. Follow this line to make the cut down to the pelvic bone. If you don't locate the cut properly, feel under the front edge of the pelvic arch for a small projection. If the knife is located directly over this bone, you'll be in the right place. On younger animals, you can cut through the pelvic bone with a sturdy, large knife. On older animals you may need to use a meat saw to cut through the pelvic bone. Be very careful, however, not to cut into the urinary tract and bladder which lies just behind and below the pelvic bone. To open the belly, position the knife, point facing outward and blade-edge down, and place your knife-holding hand inside the cut made between the hams and where the abdominal muscle begins. Cut along the centerline of the belly down to the cut made in the breastbone. As you make the cut, the intestines will fall out, hanging by their attachments to the inside of the carcass. Go back up to the rear of the hog and, using a sharp, pointed knife, cut the bung from the fat on both sides and back. Pull the loosened bung and pizzle (if a boar) down through the pelvic cut and down with the rest of the intestines, past the kidneys, loosening it from the kidney fat with the knife. Grasp the intestines at the bung with one hand, then push and pull them down and away from their backbone attachment. Run your fingers between the liver and backbone and pull it free. As the intestines fall below the diaphragm, while still holding the bung end of the intestines, cut through the diaphragm to the backbone. Make the cut encircling the entire diaphragm, loosening the heart and lungs. Make sure all attachments are cut, but be very careful not to cut into the intestines. Pull the entire offal from the carcass, cutting away any attachments from the backbone. Cut off the gullet where it goes into the throat.

The final step in gutting is to disjoint and remove the head if you have not already done so. In commercial operations the head is disjointed, leaving the jowls attached to the carcass. This is harder to do and, as I mentioned before, I prefer to remove the entire head unskinned, then skin the head out later. Make a cut encircling the head just behind the ear and at right angles to the backbone. Cut to the bone. The cut should be made at the location where the last vertebra of the neck bone meets the skull. The joint consists of a small button end of backbone fitting over the skull joint. The tendons holding the joint together looks like a hand grasping a round object such as a ball. Using a sharp knife, cut through the tendons to free the head. You will probably need to grasp the snout and an ear and twist and turn as you make the cut. Place something beneath the head to catch it when it falls free.

Thoroughly wash out the cavity with cold water. Carefully cut the gallbladder from the liver, taking care not to cut into the bladder. Cut off the auricles of the heart. Cut out the tongue. Immediately wash the heart, tongue, and liver in cold water, then place in ice water to chill. After chilling, hang up to dry, then process as desired. If you plan to render lard and, if not fouled by the intestines, peel the caul fat from the stomach and the ruffle fat from the small intestines. Wash in cold water, place in ice water to chill, and hang up to dry.

Splitting the Carcass

It's important to chill the carcass down to below 40°F as soon as possible. The carcass will chill faster and easier after splitting in half. The carcass should be split and allowed to chill twenty-four hours, or at least overnight in temperatures of 34°F to 36°F. Unlike other meats, however, pork is not improved by aging, and it deteriorates faster than other meats, so never hang pork to age.

Splitting can be done in one of two ways, depending on the tools and the desired meat cuts. The traditional, and most commonly used commercial method, is to split the backbone, or "chine," down the middle. Use a meat saw to make the cut. When you reach the bottom of the last of the backbone, have someone steady or hold the carcass to keep it from swinging. Cut through the last of the neck meat with a knife to complete the backbone separation.

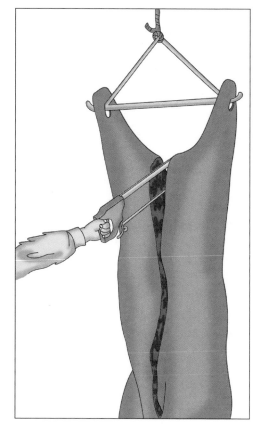

RIGHT: The carcass should be thoroughly washed with cold water, then split and allowed to chill for twenty-four hours or at least overnight in temperatures of 34°F to 36°F. The traditional method is to saw down the center of the backbone creating chops.

The country method, and the one used by our family, is to cut down either side of the backbone, leaving the backbone intact. But first, the tenderloins, located inside the carcass and next to the backbone, are removed. Make an initial cut at the bottom ends of the tenderloins and they will simply peel out. This is the most tender meat on the hog and we usually fried this delicacy the evening of butchering. The backbone makes a very savory roast cooked with potatoes. My granddad relished this part of the hog the most, picking out the succulent bone marrow. Splitting in this manner, however, is a bit more difficult to do. As you finish sawing the cut on one side of the backbone, the side of the carcass with the attached backbone becomes heavier and it will swing down. Have someone help hold the side steady. Then have your helper hold the other side steady while you cut away the backbone from that side. You can also cut out the backbone with the carcass lying on a table. Pull out the leaf fat from the inside of the rib cage and save it for lard. If you don't pull this out, the inside of the carcass may not chill out properly. Regardless of the method used, it's important to thoroughly wash the inside of the carcass, as well as the outside if needed, with cold, running water.

Cutting Up the Carcass

As I mentioned earlier, there is no single correct way of cutting up the carcass. The cutting method depends on how you intend to store and cook the meat. You may want more fresh meat, or you may wish to freeze more. You may want to cure hams, or you may desire more or less sausage. The most common cutting method, however, separates the carcass into two hams, two loins, two picnic shoulders,

BELOW: The carcass can be cut up in many different ways. The most common results in two hams, two loins, two picnic shoulders, two shoulder butts, two ribs slabs, two bacon sides, and two jowls.

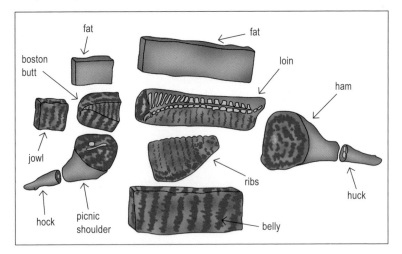

ABOVE: Lay one of the halves, skin-side down, on a sturdy worktable. Cut into shoulder, side, and ham sections.

and two shoulder butts, as well as the rib slabs, bacon sides or pork bellies, fat, and the head. If you've followed my method, the head has already been removed, and the split halves chilled properly down to 40°F. If the weather warms and the meat doesn't chill properly overnight, it's important to cut the halves into individual pieces and hang to cool or pack in ice, but this is much less safer than proper chilling. It's also important the meat stay chilled, so work in a cold or cool environment and return the meat cuts to a cool or cold area as soon as possible, or wrap and freeze immediately. I like to make all the initial cuts first, then go back and process the different cuts.

Begin the cutting process with a half of the chilled carcass lying skin-side down on a sturdy table. Using a meat saw, cut off the front hocks, then remove the shoulder by cutting between the second and third ribs. The cut should be parallel to the cut made to remove the head. After you cut through the bone, use a large butcher knife to continue the cut through the meat and skin. This creates a two-rib shoulder.

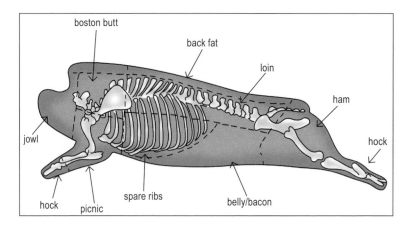

ABOVE: Separate the half into the basic cuts.

The hams can be cut as long-cut hams for country-style "aged" curing or short-cut for the more traditional short-cut ham. For information on curing hams, see *The Joy of Smoking and Salt Curing* by Monte Burch. Using a meat saw, cut off the hock before removing the ham. To create a long-cut ham, make the cut just behind the rise of the pelvic arch, and at a ninety-degree angle to the direction of the leg. To create a short-cut ham, make the cut through the second vertebra located behind the pelvic rise, again using a meat saw for the initial cuts followed by a butcher knife.

You now have the loin, rib, and bacon sections left. With a meat saw, remove the loin from the ribs and bacon, making a cut beginning just below the curve of the backbone at the shoulder end and running to the edge of the tenderloin on the ham end, sawing across the ribs. Again, finish the cut with a butcher knife. Trim the back fat from the loin, cutting around the muscle with a boning knife. Some like to leave about a fourth of the back fat on the loin, providing "juicier" pork chops. If you prefer to remove all back fat, once you make the initial cuts, simply peel the back fat strip from the loin, pulling it off with your hands. A strip of sinew divides the two. To separate the ribs from the sides, insert a thin boning knife between the end of the ribs and the side and slice and pull the ribs away from the side. Keep the knife blade edge turned toward the ribs to leave as much meat as possible on the ribs. Remove the shoulder ribs or neck bone from the shoulders in the same manner. This leaves the center or loin containing the loin, ribs, and side.

Once you have one-half of the hog made into the basic cuts, do the opposite half in the same manner. The hocks need no further processing, and can be immediately wrapped and frozen.

Trimming and Creating the Cuts

The basic meat cuts are now trimmed and further divided into the cuts desired for cooking. Have a small container on hand to hold the bloody and gristle pieces to be discarded. You'll also need containers for the trimmings to be used for sausage, and one for the fat to be rendered into lard. Regardless of how good you are at skinning or scalding, there will be some hairs on the carcass. Pick these off with your fingers or use a knife blade to scrape them off, and then wipe them off onto paper toweling.

Shoulder

The shoulder may be used in many ways. It can be ground entirely into sausage, and adds a lot to the sausage pile. Or you may divide it into your favorite cuts. The shoulder is typically divided into a pork shoulder arm or picnic, and a pork shoulder blade or Boston Butt. The shoulder is divided using a meat saw to cut through the bone, followed by a knife to finish the cut. Then trim off the fat to be used for lard.

The arm or picnic contains the arm bone, shank bone, and a portion of the blade bone as well as the shoulder muscles interspersed with fat. It can be used whole as a fresh pork roast, or cured in the manner of hams. A picnic shoulder is one of the best meats for

ABOVE: You will need a meat saw to make these cuts. Remove the front hock.

smoke-cooking as it has lots of fat running through it and creates fantastic pulled pork.

For the recipe, see *The Joy of Smoking and Salt Curing* by Monte Burch. The picnic shoulder can also be sliced into pork steaks. The blade or "Boston Butt" is the top portion of the shoulder and contains the blade bone as well as muscles and fat. It is commonly used whole as a roast.

BELOW: Remove the jowl if still attached. Remove the shoulder from the half, cutting between the second and third ribs.

Loin

The loin can be cut in several ways. Bone out and peel out the loin for a whole loin to be smoked, grilled or fried for tenderloin sandwiches. One popular cut is the double chop. This consists of the boned-out loin cut into chops about two inches thick and then butterflied or sliced almost in half, spread flat and then pounded into a large tenderloin. In days past, the center portion of the boned-out pork loin was often baked whole as a boneless roast. Or the loin can be sawed into chops, consisting of the rib ends, backbone, and loin meat. You'll probably need a powered meat saw to do this chore properly.

One of my uncles made pork chops by cutting down between the ribs to the backbone with a knife, then using a hatchet to cut the chops apart. I've tried it; skill is definitely involved, but I guess that's why they're called pork chops. The loin is commonly cut into three kinds of chops: shoulder-end or "blade" chops, center-cut chops, and ham-end or sirloin chops. The center cut produces the best chops as it also contains the tenderloin meat (if not already removed from the carcass). Some also like to cook the center portion of the pork loin whole, as a rib roast, but it does take quite a bit of freezer space if not

BELOW: Separate the ham from the loin section, using a meat saw to cut through the bone.

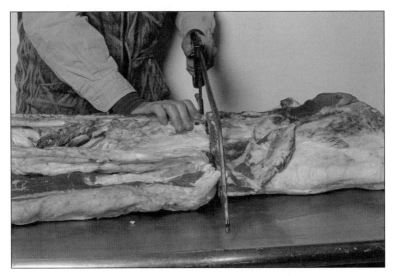

cooked fresh. Another popular cut is country-style ribs. This is made by splitting the blade end of the loin in half lengthwise and contains rib ends, backbone, and part of the loin-eye muscle.

Ham

Pork hind legs, more commonly called hams, may also be put into sausage, sliced as ham steaks, cooked fresh as roast, either bone-in or bone-out, or cured. The latter is the most common use of this meaty cut. To make a boneless ham, position the ham skin-side down and with the butt end facing you. Use a boning knife to remove the meat from around the aitchbone. Disjoint the aitch bone from the straight long-leg bone.

BELOW: The hams can be cut to create a long-cut, or short-cut ham, depending on the curing choice.

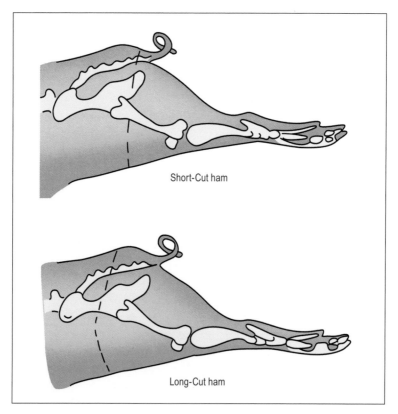

Short-Cut ham

Long-Cut ham

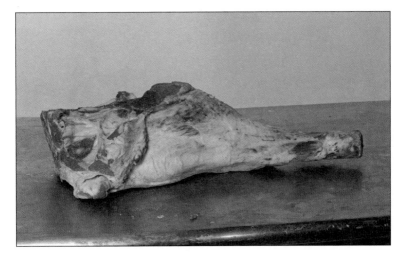

A long-cut ham for country curing and aging.

Cut through the top of the ham to remove the leg and shank bone intact. Turn the boning knife to trim around the bones as you lift them out. With all bones removed, shape the ham into a roll and tie with white butcher's string, or use a "ham net." Hams to be cured should have the cut ends trimmed and "smoothed up."

BELOW: A short-cut ham for curing.

Excess fat should also be removed, leaving about one-half-inch thickness on the butt end or skinned hams. There is a slight protrusion of the aitchbone and this should be sawn off so curing agents can be worked well around the butt end of the ham. For recipes for curing ham, see *The Joy of Smoking and Salt Curing.*

Rib

A whole pork rib slab consists of several parts, including the ribs, the cartilage (also called the brisket), the sternum, point, the skirt, and the fell or membrane. Whole ribs may be cooked as the whole slab, but are more commonly divided into the spareribs, or the bottom section, and the back ribs, or those coming from the top

BELOW: Separate the loin from the ribs and bacon by sawing just below the curve of the backbone at the shoulder end and running to the edge of the tenderloin on the ham end.

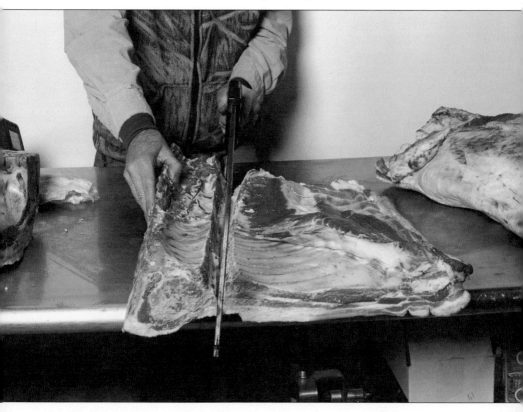

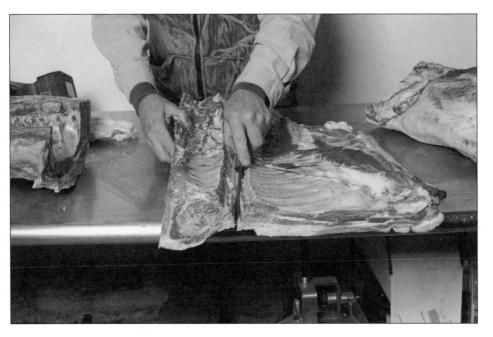

ABOVE: Finish the cut through the meat with a knife.

BELOW: Pull the leaf lard from the inside of the sides.

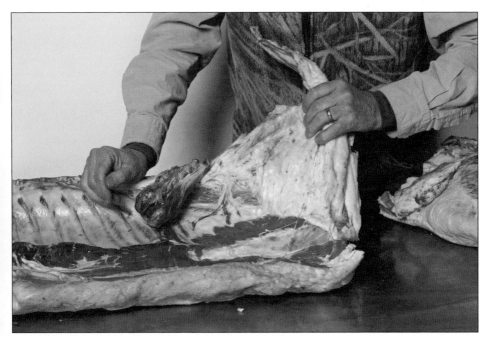

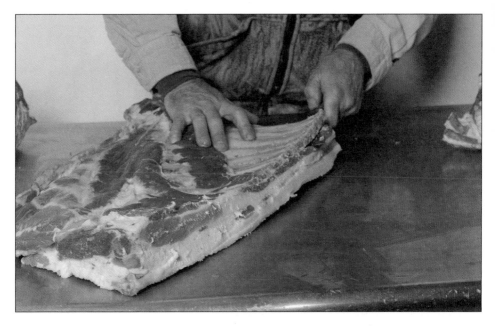

ABOVE: Remove the ribs from the sides using a boning knife. Start at the top.

BELOW: Continue cutting and peeling the ribs from the sides.

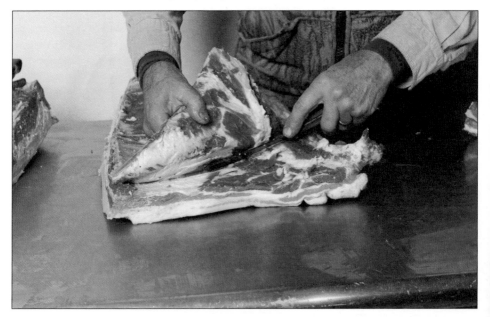

ABOVE: A second method of cutting up a carcass involves cutting down both sides of the backbone and removing it whole. The backbone is then sawed into sections for a stew pot.

BELOW: The loins and tenderloins are removed from the carcass and cooked as boneless meats.

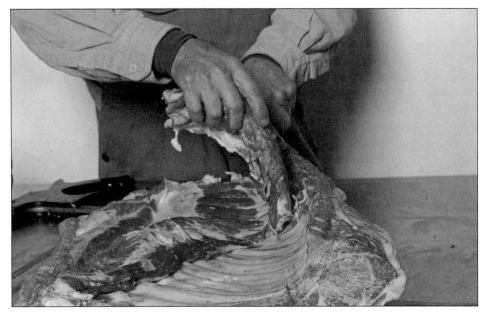

part of the rib cage, along the backbone or loin area. If the back rib slabs weigh under 1.75 pounds, they are usually called "baby-back" ribs and are one of the most expensive pork cuts. Use a meat saw and butcher knife to divide the ribs into the various parts.

Sides or Bacon

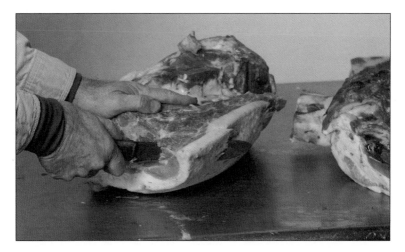

ABOVE: You are now ready to trim and finish cutting each section into usable pieces.

BELOW: As you trim out the pieces set aside the trimmings for sausage.

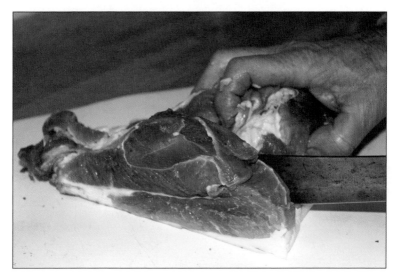

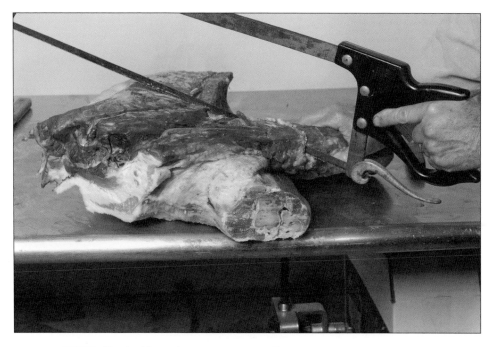

ABOVE: The shoulder can be cut into a picnic and butt.

BELOW: Or you can slice it for steaks.

LEFT: You can also bone out the shoulder and use it in sausage.

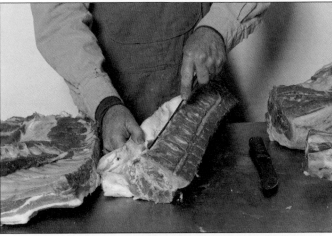

LEFT: Trim the back fat off the loin or pork chop section.

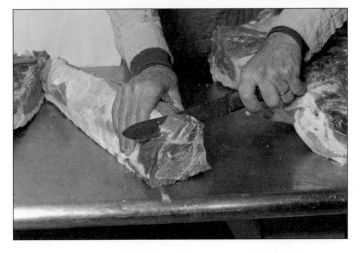

LEFT: Using a knife, cut down between the rib portions of the chops to the backbone.

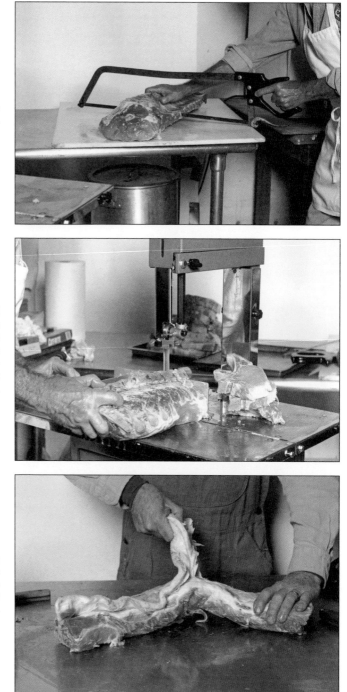

RIGHT: Finish the cut with a saw.

RIGHT: A powered meat bandsaw makes this chore much easier and allows you to cut the chops to the thickness desired, cutting through the ribs.

RIGHT: If using the boneless loin method, remove the back fat and sinew from the whole loin.

LEFT: You can also bone out the loin from the rib/backbone for a boneless loin cut.

LEFT: This again provides a loin and "backbone."

BELOW: Cut the rear hock from the ham.

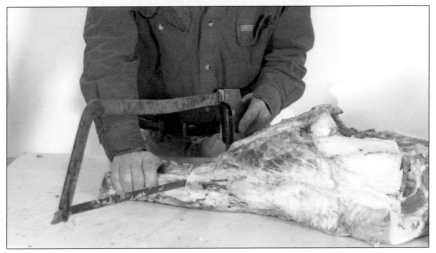

RIGHT: Trim the ham, removing excess fat and smoothing up any rough edges.

RIGHT: The resulting ham is ready to cure.

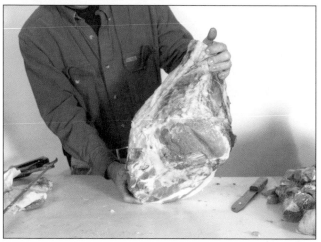

RIGHT: You can also create a boneless ham roast. Use a boning knife to follow around the bones.

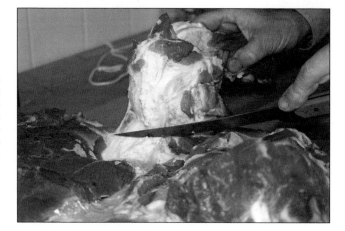

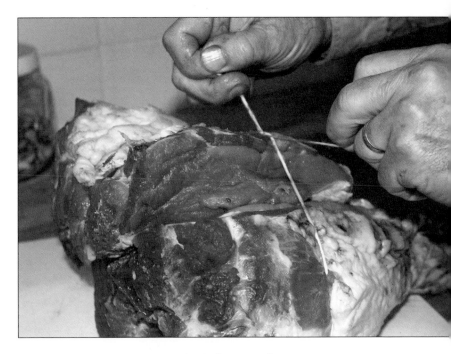

ABOVE: Tie the boned-out meat using butcher's string or a ham net.

BELOW: A whole rib consists of several parts. Cut the rib section into pieces for easier cooking.

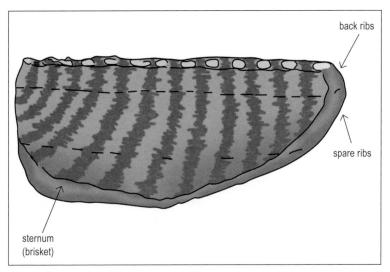

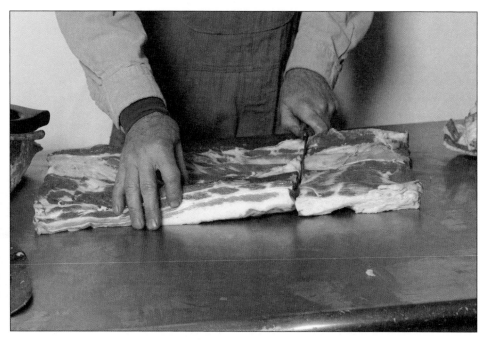

ABOVE: Trim the sides into square or rectangular pieces for curing.

BELOW: The resulting sides ready to cure.

Trim up the pork bellies or sides into nice square or rectangular shapes, and they're ready to cure into bacon. For recipes see *The Joy of Smoking and Salt Curing*.

Sausage

ABOVE: Cut the trimmings into small pieces that will fit through your sausage grinder.

BELOW: Cut away excess fat.

ABOVE: Prepare the sausage seasoning and spread over the sausage.

BELOW: Mix the cure and meat well.

ABOVE: Then grind and stuff the sausage.

Sausage is one of the favorite pork foods, either fresh or used in summer and other cooked sausages. In fact, fresh sausage was considered the reward for the butchering chores, with fresh sausage burgers the "sample" for the second night of butchering. As you trim the cuts of meat, the trimmings go into the sausage pot. A side, shoulder, or even ham can also be added if you prefer more sausage. Sausage, however, doesn't keep very long in the freezer before it loses its taste, so don't overdo it. We also like to keep our sausage fairly lean, so we don't include a lot of the fatty pieces. The common ratio is about one-third fat and two-thirds lean. If the sausage is too fatty, there will be a lot of cooking loss. If it's too lean, the patties will be hard and dry. We grind a batch of the meat trimmings, add the salt and spices, and then sample. Although not allowed in commercial sausage, we usually add the heart to the sausage pot as well. The skinned tongue could also be added. Make sure you keep the sausage trimmings cold or below

40°F until you're ready to make sausage. When you have all the cures, spices, gear, and casings ready to make sausage, cut the trimmings into small cubes or strips that will readily go through your sausage grinder. Sausage recipes are available in my book *The Complete Guide to Sausage Making*.

Liver

The liver should be kept chilled until it can be sliced and packaged. Liver is kind of slippery and rubbery and hard to slice properly. One trick is to place it on a wax paper-lined flat pan or cookie sheet and place in the freezer for about an hour, or until the meat just starts to harden. It is then easy to consistently slice. Wrap in freezer paper, date, and freeze.

Brains and Head

The brains were also a delicacy relished by the old-timers. The skull was sawn down the middle and the brains scooped out. They were washed thoroughly, then cooked, or more often cooked with scrambled eggs, one of my grandmother's favorite dishes. The head meat also can be made into another old-time favorite, headcheese. The ears and eyes are removed from the split head, along with the brains. The nasal passages are cleaned out and the teeth chopped off. The bony head pieces are placed in a large pot or kettle, covered with water, and allowed to simmer until the meat falls off the bones. The meat and bones are then strained through a kitchen strainer, and the meat picked off. Salt and pepper is added to the meat, along with a little of the strained liquid. The meat mixture is simmered until it thickens, then poured into a glass pan and refrigerated. When cooled it is sliced like lunch meats and served on sandwiches. To make scrapple, the meat and some strained broth are cooked with cornmeal added. When thick, the mixture is again poured into a loaf pan and refrigerated. When chilled and set, the scrapple is sliced and fried for breakfast. Serve with butter and syrup.

Lard

Lard was the cooking oil of the old-timers until it became a health concern. Lard or rendered pig fat is a saturated fat, meaning all the fatty acid molecules are filled with hydrogen atoms. These saturated

ABOVE: Even a "modern" hog has quite a bit of fat. You can render the fat into lard for cooking. The first step is to cut the fat into one-inch cubes.

BELOW: A large cooking pot and gas cooker such as a turkey fryer works well for rendering lard.

ABOVE: Slowly heat and cook the fat until the lard is rendered from the fat. Stir continually to prevent sticking and burning.

ABOVE: Pour off the liquefied fat. You can pour it through a cloth strainer or bag.

ABOVE: A sausage stuffer does double-duty as a lard press.

BELOW: As the fat renders out, the cracklings will turn brown and float.

ABOVE: The cracklings are considered a delicacy while fresh.

fats are considered bad for you because they can contribute to heart disease. Recent findings, however, indicate some amounts of saturated fats from pastured animals, not from grain-fed animals, may in fact be good for you.

In any case, a lot of fat is available from butchering even a lean hog. This fat can be rendered into lard, but I warn you, the chore takes time and effort. In the old days, one or two people were assigned to render the lard during butchering days. The lard was rendered in huge iron kettles over a wood fire, continually stirred and watched so it wouldn't burn, then the liquid skimmed off and run through a lard press, which had a cloth bag to catch the solid fat and meat pieces. The lard press squeezed out the liquid and the remaining solid skin, fat and meat pieces called the "cracklings" were left. Hot out of the kettle, these delicacies were a favorite during butchering days. If you can find a lard kettle and press, you're in luck. However, I have found rendering lard is much easier using a large turkey fryer pot and burner. You'll need a wooden stick for stirring the fat as it is rendered. Although the old-timers used all the fat, including the caul and ruffle fats, these fats tend to produce darker lard and our family never used them. Cut the fat into small, approximately one-inch cubes before rendering. This allows the chunks of fat to heat quickly and evenly. Place a handful or two of the fat pieces in the kettle or pot to start melting, and then gradually add the remaining pieces. Do not overfill the pot as it will boil over and can create a dangerous fire. Keep the fire low throughout the entire process to prevent scorching the fat pieces. Continually stir the fat pieces to keep them from sticking, especially at the start. The temperature of the lard will reach about 212°F as it begins to render. As the water in the fat molecules is cooked out, the temperature will rise. Do not allow the temperature to get above 225°F. This is one chore that takes patience and constant attention so you might as well get your favorite lawn chair. As the fat renders out, the cracklings will begin to turn brown and float. Once they are nearly rendered of all fat, they will then fall to the bottom. Make sure to continue stirring at this time to prevent them from sticking. Our family removed the lard from the fire when all the cracklings floated, although the fat was not totally rendered from them. It was much safer than possibly burning the lard with a too hot wood fire in those days. Once you're satisfied the lard is rendered properly, allow the lard to cool slightly and settle. Dip the lard out and pour it through a kitchen strainer with a layer of cheesecloth. Place the hot lard immediately into containers and store at a temperature near or below freezing. This allows the lard to set up properly into a smooth buttery texture. Lard can be stored in containers unfrozen, but they must be tightly sealed. Air and light creates a chemical change that turns lard rancid. If the moisture has been properly eliminated during the rendering, lard should, however, keep a long time. Excess lard can also be frozen.

Preservation

Fresh pork is extremely perishable, and must be kept refrigerated at temperatures of 34°F to 36°F but should not be stored longer than three to five days. Fresh pork may be preserved by freezing, curing, and canning. For more information on curing pork, see *The Joy of Smoking and Salt Curing*.

⑤

Beef

BUTCHERING A BEEF is the ultimate experience for the home butcher. A beef provides a lot of meat, but also takes a lot of work, some special tools, and a bit more skill. But once you learn the steps, you'll find, as with all home butchering, it's fairly easy. The first consideration is the size and weight of the animal. You'll need a sturdy meat pole and hoist. Many years ago when I attempted butchering my first beef, my dad drove from his home, forty-five miles away, to help me. At the time I had an old Ford 8N tractor: not the most powerful, but affordable.

A huge oak behind our house had a big limb I'd used for hanging deer, so we decided to hang the beef there as well. A snowstorm followed by some melting and then refreezing covered the ground with patches of ice. I killed the calf, hooked a chain to the gambrel, threw it over the tree limb, and proceeded to use the tractor to hoist the calf in place. With the calf about halfway up, the tractor wheels hit a patch of ice and began spinning, stopping the upward movement of the carcass. The ice was thin and I figured the wheels would dig through, so I poured the gas to the old tractor. I was right, the wheels dug through, the tractor leaped forward and before I could get my foot on the brake, the calf went up and over the tree limb, then crashed to

ABOVE: Butchering a beef requires more effort and tools, mostly due to the size of the animal. These days, grass-fed beef are extremely popular because the meat is leaner.

the ground with a loud thump. "Heck of a way to tenderize the meat," my dad quipped. Many years later, as Dad was nearing the end, he began laughing one day. "Remember how you tenderized that beef?" As with butchering a hog, working up a beef is much easier with two working together.

Choosing

The choices in beef are also varied, and somewhat different from the past. In the past, the most popular beef was "corn fed," and corn-fed beef is still the most commonly served meat. Corn-fed beef is high in saturated fats, and high consumption is considered a heart health hazard. Grass-fed beef, however, is becoming increasingly more popular. The meat is leaner, higher in omega-3 fatty acids and has more cancer-fighting fat, or conjugated linoleic acid (CLA). Grass-fed beef, eaten in moderation, may in fact be good for you. Corn-fed beef does have higher amounts of marbling than grass fed. There will be small, but easily seen flecks of marbling throughout a cross section of the meat, and especially in the "eye" of the loin and ribs. The meat will be a bright cherry red, and a smooth layer of white fat will cover the dressed carcass. A grass-fed beef will have less marbling fat and the fat will tend to be slightly yellow. Actually this indicates more carotene, another health benefit. The lean portions of the meat will also be somewhat softer. Tenderness, however, is more due to the age and breed rather than the feed. Again, if you raise your own, you have control of your food. For instance, we run a beef cow-calf operation on our farm. We do not use any type of growth hormones or chemicals in raising our beef. We have what is called a "closed herd," meaning we've raised almost all of the animals through several generations for

BELOW: Choosing the correct breed and age is important for quality beef. A young beef breed animal is the best choice.

quality, health, and, just as important, attitude. We sell the majority of the calves to the market, but keep back some for beef and some replacement heifers. They are all grass fed with hay in the winter and no grain or additives.

The breed of the animal also affects the quality and taste of the meat. Cattle are raised as either beef or dairy breeds, with a number of breeds in each group. As a general rule, the beef breeds are the best meat choice. They tend to be thicker fleshed and will fatten better and quicker with more fat over the lean muscles. There is also usually less waste in internal fats than the dairy breeds. I'm not saying you shouldn't utilize a dairy breed, just be aware they don't dress out as well. A properly finished beef breed will have meatier roasts and steaks than a finished dairy breed. For those who keep a dairy cow for home milk production, one method used for many years is to breed the milk cow to one of the beef breeds, producing a cross-bred calf for meat. The different breeds even in their groups also have varying meat qualities, as witness the advertising concerning the Angus breeds. Incidentally, we raise Angus cross breeds, or what's commonly called "black baldies." They produce a high-dressing carcass and are the top-selling breed at the sale barns.

Age is also important. Meat from cattle can be veal or beef. Veal is the meat from calves three months or younger and weighing 350 pounds or less. They are basically "milk fed" with very little roughage. Veal is a very fine-grained meat, somewhat soft and velvety in texture. It is a light pink in color, and is extremely lean with very little fat. Veal, as you can guess, is fairly expensive and usually not available except in butcher shops.

The most common beef calf for butchering is a yearling to eighteen months, and sometimes a two-year-old. The meat from either a steer or heifer of this age is at its prime tenderness, yet produces a good butcher-sized carcass. The meat from older animals tends to be tougher. I've butchered older cows at times, and they can be butchered, but also tend to have a lot more fat surrounding the meat and are tougher. For those who butcher older animals, most of the meat is made into hamburger.

If you are feeding out your own butcher calf, consider grass-raised. They will finish out good without excessive internal caul and ruffle fat.

Killing

Killing a calf is not a pleasant or easy chore, especially if you've raised it. Pen the animal by itself the day before slaughtering. Hold feed for twenty-four hours before butchering, but supply plenty of water. Have everything on hand for the butchering, including a heavy-duty hoist and meat pole. It's important to kill the animal as quickly and humanely as possible. Do not allow the animal to get excited by running it around or whipping it. This causes the blood to flush into the system and also an increase in lactic acid. Both create insufficient bleeding, and excessively bloody meat. Secure the animal's head so you can stun it properly without the animal moving around. A head-gate or chute with a drop-down side is a good choice. The animal can be stunned by using a mechanical stunner or shooting. In days past,

BELOW: The animal is stunned using a mechanical stunner or by shooting. Old-timers stunned using a heavy hammer or sledge. The stunning point is shown.

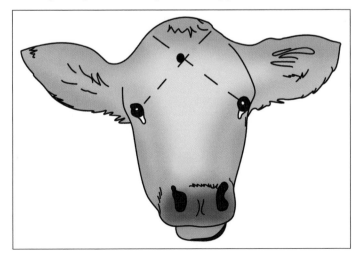

old-timers stunned with a hard blow using a heavy axe head or hammer, but it takes skill. Using a mechanical stunner is the best method, but they are somewhat expensive for occasional use. The animal could be shot to immobilize it, but putting a calf down is not easy. Some use larger caliber guns than a .22, and some say a shotgun with a slug does the job best. The gun should be held within twelve inches or so to the skull and the point to strike or shoot is not between the eyes, as is often thought, but just to one side of an intersection from the right horn (or poll) to the left eye and from the left poll to the right eye.

Bleeding

The animal must be bled immediately after it has been stunned. Standing behind the animal and away from the legs, use a sharp sticking knife to make a thrusting cut through the middle of the

BELOW: The animal is then "stuck" using a sharp knife to sever the carotid artery. Some like to cut the throat to ensure more rapid bleeding.

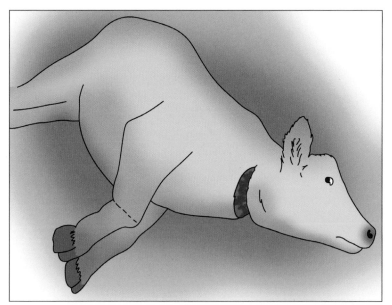

dewlap and just in front of the breastbone. With the point of the knife facing the rear of the animal, push the knife beneath the breast-bone and toward the animal's rump. Continue pushing to make a cut toward the backbone in order to cut the arteries crossing just beneath the front point of the breastbone. Do not, however, cut deep enough into the chest cavity and cut the heart, as this will stop the heart from pumping blood. Pumping a foreleg back and forth will help pump out the blood. You may wish to catch the blood for specialty blood dishes.

Skinning

The skinning and gutting of a beef carcass can be done in several ways. The method described is the way I learned. A beef carcass can be skinned while hanging, but because of the size, the best tactic is to do some skinning before hoisting, then hoist and finish skinning and gutting. Prop the animal on its back with a pritch pole or sturdy stick with sharpened ends. You may wish to have two, one for each side.

BELOW: Using a pritch pole or a sturdy stick sharpened on both ends, prop the carcass on its back. Make a shallow cut just through the skin from the anus to the throat and then on the inside of each hind leg.

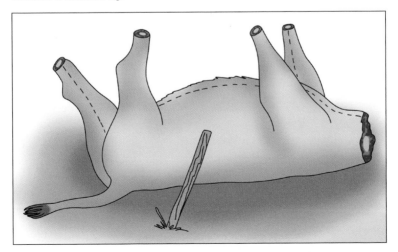

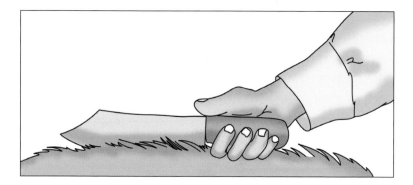

ABOVE: Make the cut on the belly very shallow—just through the skin and not into the abdominal muscles.

Make a cut on the back of the legs, between the dewclaws and hoofs, to release the tendon. Split the skin on the inside of the legs. The next step, splitting the skin on the belly, must be done very carefully. Using a knife held flat to the skin, slice through the skin from the bung area to the throat cut. You can also use a skinning knife with a gut hook for the chore. It's extremely important not to cut into the paunch area.

After this cut has been made, continue the cuts made on the inside of the legs to the centerline cut. Skin the forelegs. To remove the feet and shanks, locate and cut through the flat "knee" joint, bending the

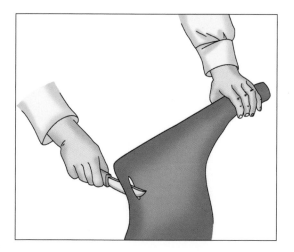

LEFT: Remove the feet. Cut between the large tendons on the back legs to insert a gambrel.

joint to locate properly. Work the knife around the joint in order to sever the tendons. Repeat the steps for the hind legs, relaxing the tendons, and then skinning.

Remove the hind feet and shanks by sawing with a meat saw just below the hocks or relax the tendons, and locate the lowest joint of the hock. Cut around it with a knife, and then snap the leg sideways and it will usually break apart fairly easily. Insert a sharp knife behind the hocks to divide the large tendons on the back. This will be the location for the gambrel used to hoist the carcass.

At this point, I like to remove the head, although some will leave the head in place until after skinning and gutting, and skin the head along with the carcass. Remove the head by cutting through the atlas joint, located at the base of the skull, or beginning just behind the poll and continuing around the head, cutting through the neck meat and the gullet. You will probably have to twist and turn the head around to cut through the tendons surrounding the joint. Set the head aside for now in a cold place to skin later. Continue with the remainder of the skinning process.

BELOW: You can also remove the head at this time, setting it aside to skin later.

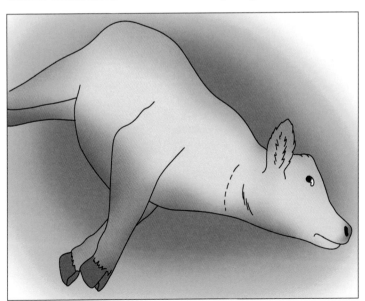

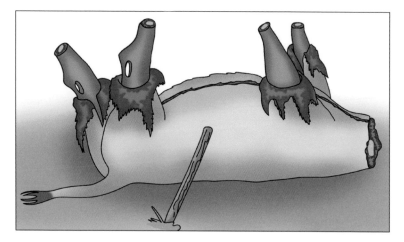

ABOVE: Starting where the feet were removed, skin the front and rear legs down to the sides.

The next step is called "siding" and involves removing the remainder of the skin from and down the sides. You'll need a good, sharp skinning knife, or a knife with a well-rounded drop-point. Grasping the skin at the cut line on the belly and brisket with one hand, use the knife in a sweeping motion to cut the hide away from the carcass. Use your other hand to help pull the skin away. Continue down over the sides as far as you can reach. This is the hardest part of the skinning chore. As you skin to the legs, continue skinning them out as well, but do not skin the outside of the rounds or rear.

Gutting

Once you've skinned down the sides as far as you can, you're ready to open the carcass and begin gutting. Using a knife held flat, cut through the meat down the center of the breastbone, but do not cut past the point of the breastbone. Use a meat saw to cut through the breastbone. Hold the knife point up, with the blade facing toward the rear of the animal. Use your hand to push the intestines and paunch down and out of the way, and at the same time cut through the abdom-

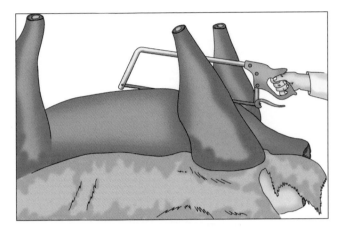

ABOVE: Using a knife to make the initial cut, cut through the meat in the center of the breastbone, and then finish with a meat saw.

inal wall. Be extremely careful not to cut into the entrails or paunch. Remove the penis (if a steer), as well as the testicles if it is a bull. The inside of the rounds or hind legs are covered with a fairly thick membrane. Find the centerline of the membrane and cut down to the pelvic bone. On young animals you can usually separate the pelvic bone by cutting through the cartilage. On older animals, you will need to use a meat saw to cut through the bone.

BELOW: Open the paunch by making a starting cut at the breastbone, inserting your hand with the knife blade outward and cutting toward the anus, pushing the paunch and intestines down and away as you make the cut.

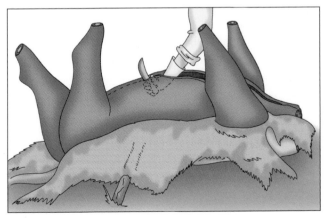

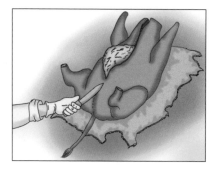

ABOVE: Cut down through the center of the rounds, following the centerline membrane to the pelvic arch, and then cut through the arch.

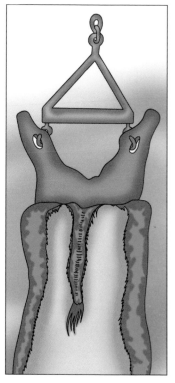

RIGHT: Hoist the carcass and continue skinning the rounds and remove the tail.

You're now ready to hoist the carcass and continue the gutting and skinning. Insert the single-tree or beef gambrel into the cuts made in the hind legs. Hoist the beef up until you can reach the rounds. Skin the rounds and the back portion near the rounds; again use your knife to make sweeping cutting motions between the hide and the flesh, pulling the hide with your other hand. Skin out the tail and cut it off. Place the tail in cold water.

As you hoist the carcass, the paunch will fall downward, but the intestines are held by the bung and inside attachments. Use a pointed sharp knife to cut around the bung on the sides and back. Pull the bung down and out through the opened pelvic arch. Some butchers like to tie off the bung to help prevent fecal contamination. Pull down on the bung and the intestines will continue to fall, but will be held by the interior attachments. Hoist the carcass until it clears the ground, and then place a large tub under the carcass to catch the viscera. Continue pulling down on the bung and paunch while cutting the attachments holding the intestines in place.

Be careful not to cut into the kidneys or tenderloins. Do not allow the liver to fall out with the paunch, but cut it free as it appears. Carefully remove the gallbladder and then place the liver in a pan of cold water. Cut through the diaphragm, the thin muscle and white connective tissue sheet separating the heart and lungs from the intestines and paunch, and remove the heart and lungs. Cut through the large blood vessel of the heart (the aorta) that is attached to the backbone. Then pull out the heart, lungs, and remaining gullet section all at once. Place the heart in a pan of ice-cold water to soak. Wash the inside of the carcass with plenty of cold, running water. Examine the inside of the carcass for any abscesses or inflammations that might cause health problems with consuming the meat. If you find

RIGHT: Cut around the bung and tie it off. Pulling down on the bung, loosen the interior attachments and the intestines will fall down and forward. Cut around the skirt, or diaphragm, and allow the lungs, heart, and the remainder of the intestines to fall out. Finish the skinning process.

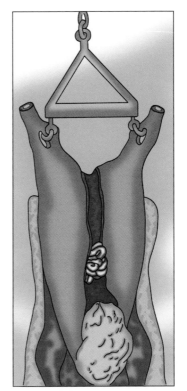

problems and are unsure of the safety of the meat, have a veterinarian examine the carcass.

If you really want to be independent, you can make your own soap from the tallow or caul and ruffle fat found around the intestines and stomach. If the fat is not fouled during the gutting, peel off and cut away, then wash and hang up to dry. The old-timers also made tripe from the first and second stomachs, cutting off the two stomachs, turning them inside-out and emptying their contents, then washing thoroughly and hanging up to drain.

Skin out the head by making a cut along the back of the poll, and continue the cut around the sides to the throat. Make a cut from the poll cut to either side of the nostril. Using a skinning knife to loosen the hide, remove the skin from the front and sides of the head down to under the chin. Wash with cold, running water to remove any blood, hairs, and regurgitated food. Remove the cheek meat by cutting down to the bone on each jaw. Remove the tongue by first making an incision on the inside of the bottom of each jaw. Then cut through the cartilage at the base of the tongue and pull it out. Scrape off any food particles and place in cold water. If you wish, split the skull and remove the brains. Wash and place all in cold water to chill.

Splitting the Carcass

The carcass must be split to properly chill quickly and also to age. Using a meat saw, start the cut on the inside, through the sacral vertebrae and down through the pelvic area. Continue sawing until you reach the rib cage area and then finish sawing the remainder of the carcass from the outside or back. Do not cut entirely through the neck so the carcass will remain balanced on the gambrel or singletree. Cut away any meat areas that are bloody, bruised, or may be contaminated or soiled. Again, wash thoroughly with cold, running water.

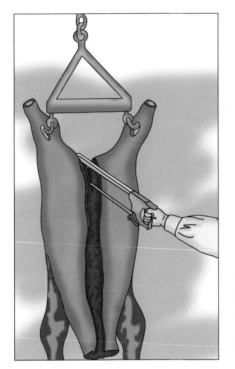

LEFT: Split the carcass down the center of the backbone using a meat saw. Leave the meat at the neck attached to prevent the sides from swinging.

Aging

Beef is usually aged before it is cut up. Aging must be done at temperatures below 40°F, and in an area safe from pests and weather. The amount of aging time depends on the age of the animal, and the amount of fat covering. Younger animals, with less fat covering, require less aging, usually from three to five days. Older animals and those with more fat covering require more aging, up to seven days. Some folks like to age beef for ten to fifteen days, but you do stand more of a chance for microbial and mold growth. If the temperature rises above 40°F, there is a chance for spoilage. It's extremely important to chill the meat to below 40°F as quickly as possible and hold the meat at temperatures between 32°F and 34°F for the amount of aging time desired to prevent bacteria growth that can spoil the meat.

Packers chill the carcass to an internal temperature of 40°F within twenty-four hours. This is not always possible for the home butcher. Some folks like to wrap the carcass with a wet sheet, clean white muslin, or large game bag. This not only improves the carcass appearance by smoothing the exterior fat, but it also offers some protection in case there is below 32°F or freezing weather. Wrap the cloth tightly around the carcass and secure it with skewers or snap ties to hold it in place. The area to hang the carcass should have plenty of air circulation to prevent mold growth.

Cutting

Cutting up a beef carcass may appear daunting, but it needn't be. As with any type of home butchering, there is no absolutely correct way to cut up the carcass. How you cut up your beef depends on how you wish to store the meat, and how you wish to prepare and serve it. For instance we bone out a good deal of the meat. We cook the bones, pick the meat off, and freeze the meat and broth for soups. This saves a lot of freezer space. There are, however, general methods used to produce the cuts conforming to most retail cuts, or those more readily recognized and also described in cookbooks.

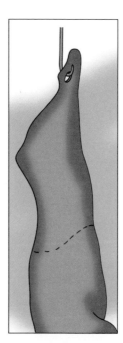

RIGHT: Beef halves are cut up into traditional cuts. The first step in cutting up is to divide the sides into quarters. Cut between the twelfth and thirteenth ribs to separate the front and rear quarters.

Quartering

The first step is to cut the sides into quarters—forequarters and hindquarters. When you make the cuts to quarter a hanging beef, you will need help to catch, hold, and carry the quarters to a cutting table. On large animals, separate the quarters while the half is still hanging; on small animals, the quarters can be easily carried to a table. Cut between the neck to separate the halves, but be careful of the swinging beef half as you finish the cut. In packer plants the carcass is transferred to hanging hooks for each half so they won't swing down when separated, and when removing the forequarters.

To remove a forequarter, make a cut between the twelfth and thirteenth rib, counting up from the neck. Insert the knife blade halfway between the flank, or front of the carcass, and the backbone and cut to the backbone between the ribs. Reverse the knife and cut between the ribs and through the cartilage at the end of the ribs. Leave the flank meat uncut until you saw through the backbone. Have someone catch and hold the quarter as you cut through the backbone. Then finish the flank-meat cut to remove the forequarter and place it on a cutting table. Some folks prefer to remove the prime rib while the forequarter is still attached, and this will cut down on the weight of the quarter.

BELOW: The quarters are then sliced into their individual cuts.

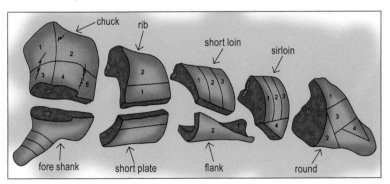

When butchering a beef, you'll cut up each quarter as you separate it, mostly due to size but also the time involved. Leave the remainder of the carcass hanging in the cold area. Have a tub or container ready for hamburger parts, as well as one for scraps and bone pieces. If saving the fat for tallow, you'll also need a container to hold the fat as you trim the meat. You'll also need paper towels or clean rags and water on hand.

Forequarter

Lay the forequarter on a table with the bone up so you can identify the cuts. The forequarter cuts are the prime rib, chuck, foreshank, plate, and neck. The first step is to remove the prime rib. Count five ribs from the front of the forequarter, and then make a cut separating the fifth and sixth ribs. Cut through the cartilage of the ribs and breastbone with a saw. Then go back and finish removing the section by cutting through the backbone with the meat saw. The section removed contains the prime rib and plate cuts. To separate these cuts, saw on a line 1.5 inches below the rib eye muscle on the quartered end and parallel to the backbone.

BELOW: The first step is to lay a beef side or quarter bone side up on a sturdy table. Following the bone structure helps determine the various cuts.

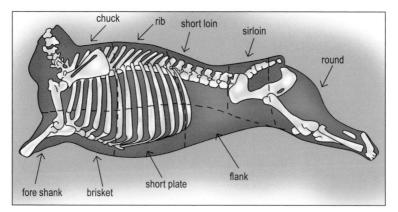

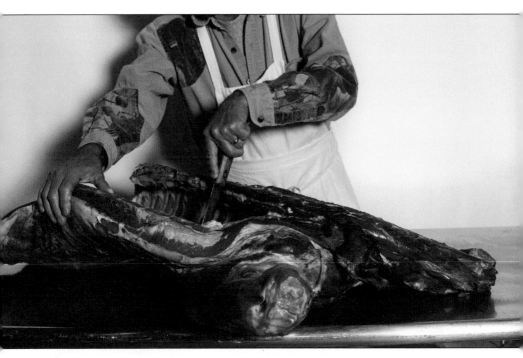

ABOVE: Remove the prime rib section, cutting between the fifth and sixth ribs.

BELOW: Locate with a knife and finish with a saw.

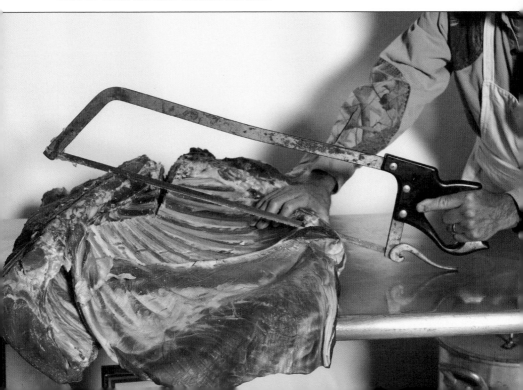

PLATE

The plate is often cut into short ribs, making cuts about two inches apart across the ribs. Or, the ribs may be boned out to create a rolled plate roast, or the meat used for stew meat. In many instances the plate is boned out for hamburger meat.

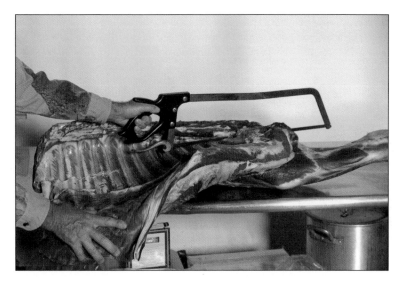

ABOVE: Separate the prime rib and plate cuts by sawing on a line 1.5 inches below the rib eye muscle and parallel to the backbone.

BELOW: Front quarter—basic cuts.

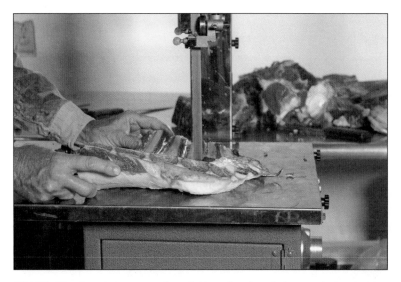

ABOVE: The plate can be cut into short ribs, boned out for rolled roast or for hamburger.

RIB EYE

The rib eye can be divided by cutting to create a large end and small end roast. They can be cooked as standing rib roasts, or as rib pot roast. The rib eye can also be sawed into rib steaks. Or you can bone out the rib eye to create a rolled roast or boneless rib steaks.

BELOW: Divide the rib eye into roasts or saw into rib steaks.

FOREARM

The forearm is removed from the chuck by making a cut with a meat saw approximately two inches above the top of the arm bone joint, and cutting parallel to the brisket. Cut with a knife between the forearm and plate to finish removing. The forearm is sawed into soup bones, or boned out for hamburger.

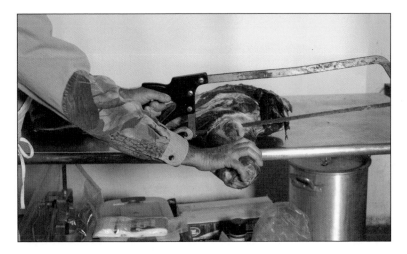

ABOVE: Remove the forearm from the chuck about two inches above the arm bone joint. Use as soup bones or bone out for hamburger.

BRISKET

Continue the cut on the same line as removing the forearm through the ribs and cartilage to remove the brisket from the chuck. A layer of fat and fascia covers the breast cut. Create a starting cut along one edge with a knife, and then peel off the fat and fascia. This

BELOW: Divide the remaining breast piece into brisket, plate, and short ribs.

long breast piece can be further divided into a brisket and plate, and the plate cut into short ribs. The boned-out brisket may be used as BBQ brisket, a roast, burgers, or often may be made into corned beef.

NECK

Cut the neck from the chuck, using a large knife to start, followed by a meat saw to cut through the vertebrae. The boned-out neck is ground into hamburger.

ABOVE: Remove the neck, and bone it out for hamburger.

CHUCK

The square-cut chuck can be used in several ways, either as steaks or roasts. The chuck is one of the tougher cuts and is most commonly used as pot roasts. Using a meat saw and knife to finish, cut the chuck into roasts of the desired thickness.

BELOW: Cut the chuck into roasts of the desired thickness.

Hindquarter

The hindquarter cuts are: short loin, flank, loin end, rump, round, and hock. Lay the hindquarter on a worktable, bones facing up so you can locate the positions of the cuts.

FLANK

The first step is to remove the flank meat, cutting it loose with a knife. Make the cut starting at the beginning of the round or leg swell, but be careful not to cut into the round muscle. Continue the cut to about two inches below the loin eye muscle on the thirteenth rib. Peel out the flank steak, a predominant muscle, and leave the remaining flank to be ground into hamburger.

BELOW: Lay the hindquarter on a table, bones facing up, and remove the flank meat with a knife. Then cut the flank steak from the flank.

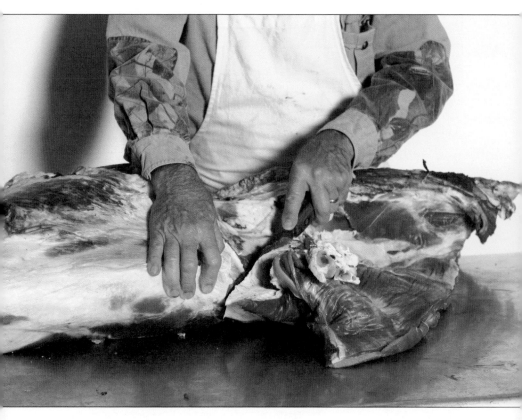

LOIN

Remove the kidney knob and surrounding fat by cutting free with a knife and pulling it away. This may be saved for tallow. Using a meat saw, make a cut starting at about the fourth sacral vertebrae, or about halfway between the tail head and the rise of the pelvic arch. Cut to the location of the beginning of the flank cut on the round. After sawing through the bones, finish the cut with a knife. The loin is usually sawed into steaks. Separate the loin into a short loin and long loin, making the cut across the loin at the cartilaginous end of the hip bone. Cut the steaks to your desired thickness. The steaks are best done with a meat bandsaw, although a handsaw with a sharp blade can be used. Beginning at the sirloin end, make a cut to remove the sirloin tip. This can be used to make sirloin tip steaks, as cube

BELOW: Remove the suet.

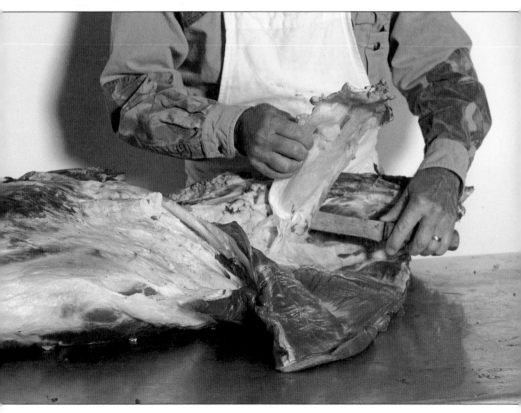

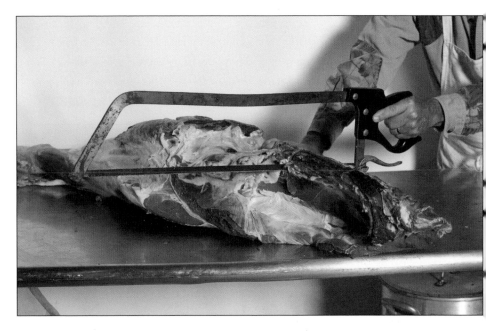

ABOVE: Remove the short loin.

BELOW: Separate the hindquarter loin (or sirloin) and round by cutting about halfway between the tail and the pelvic arch rise.

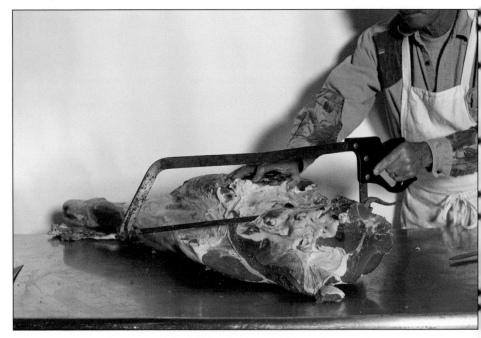

ABOVE: Cut into steaks at the desired thickness.

steaks or a sirloin tip roast. Then cut the loin into steaks, beginning at the sirloin end. The first steaks will be sirloins, followed by porterhouse, T-bones and club steaks. Or you can debone the loin creating filet mignon or tenderloin steaks from the sirloin end, and top loin steaks from the small end of the loin.

RUMP AND ROUND

Remove the rump from the round using a knife and saw as needed. Then make a cut starting at the beginning of the rump cut and continuing to the bottom of the shank. Remove the shank or hock. This

BELOW: Remove the rump from the round.

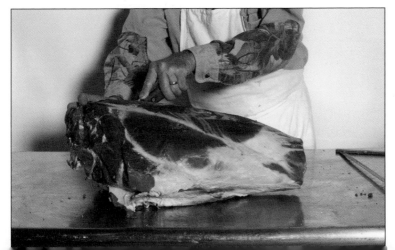

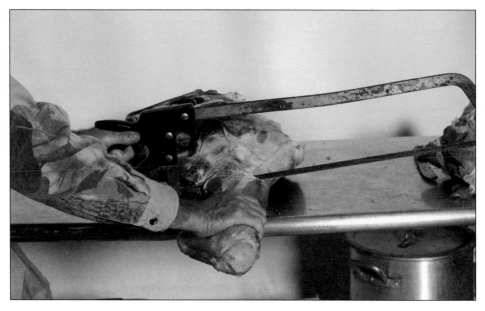

ABOVE: Remove the hind hock or shank, bone it out, or cut into smaller pieces for soup bones or stew meat.

BELOW: Three cuts are made to the round, producing the inside, outside, and heel. These can be used as roasts or round steaks.

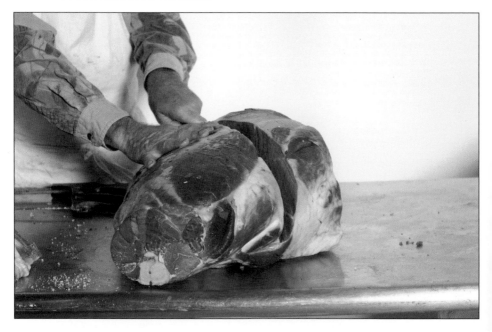

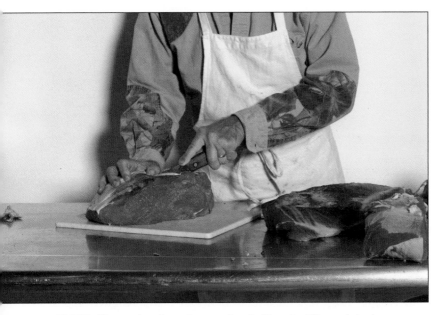

ABOVE: The round can be cut into round steaks. They should be tenderized.

creates three cuts: the inside, outside, and heel of the round. These can be used as roasts, boned out and tied into rolled roasts, or cut into round steaks. Or, you can bone out and grind for hamburger. The hind shank is also cut into smaller pieces for stew or soup meat. The skinned-out tail, which has been set aside, can also be cut into oxtail pieces for soup.

Hamburger

The trimmings, as well as those cuts selected for hamburger, should be trimmed of excess fat, then ground. One advantage of butchering your own is you can create quality ground meat, without the addition of fat, or in some cases ice, to add bulk to the meat. Make sure you wear food-safe gloves when grinding, handling, and packaging ground meat.

ABOVE: The trimmings and other portions selected are ground into hamburger.

Packaging and Storage

The meat should be packaged as quickly as possible and frozen. Take care, however, in trying to freeze a large quantity of meat in a home freezer. Make sure the freezer is operating properly. Use a thermometer inside the freezer to determine the temperature. If it has a quick-freeze compartment, use that for the initial freezing period. Use only freezer wrap paper to package the meat. Place the meat in the center of a piece of paper, fold over the sides, fold the ends over the sides, and secure with tape. Use plastic wrap, freezer paper, or wax paper between steaks before wrapping them. Remove any sharp bones from meat cuts, or cover with extra pieces of butcher paper. Make sure you label each package with the date, number of pieces,

ABOVE: Hamburger can easily be packaged with a sausage stuffer and purchased, pre-labeled bags.

and the name of the cut. Meat processed at a slaughterhouse is packaged in freezer wrap. At home you can add another layer of waxed paper or plastic wrap to further guard your meat against freezer burn.

Sheep, goats, and domestic rabbits are popular meats with homesteaders because they're easy to grow. And they're fairly easy to butcher.

⑥
Other Meats

OTHER DOMESTIC LIVESTOCK meats include mutton or lamb, goats, and rabbits. Lamb or mutton is popular with many cultures, and goat meat has also become increasingly popular, mostly due to the increased interest in "meat" goats. In fact, worldwide, goat is the most common meat. Rabbits are another popular "homestead" meat. Although not as popular in the United States, domestic rabbit is a traditional staple meat in many countries.

Sheep

Sheep are an extremely important livestock for many cultures. Not only do they provide wool and hides, but meat as well.

Choosing
The meat from sheep is classified according to age. Lamb meat is from sheep that are less than one year old. The better quality meats come from animals that are six to eight months of age. The most popular are "spring lambs," those born in the spring months of March

and April and slaughtered in November or December. Meat from slaughtered sheep older than one year is called mutton. Mutton is less popular in the United States, but is extremely popular in European countries. Mutton does have an acquired taste.

The color of lamb meat is a light pinkish-red. Mutton has a deeper red color and has more fat which provides a stronger flavor. Mutton is also less tender than lamb. If purchasing, mutton is less expensive than lamb and the cuts are larger.

Killing

Killing should be done as quickly and humanely as possible. Withhold food for twelve hours before slaughter, but provide plenty of water. Pen and catch the animal with as little stress as possible.

BELOW: The most humane means of killing is slitting the animal's throat. Cut the head off at this time. A killing and skinning cradle makes it easier to kill and skin lambs and to skin goats.

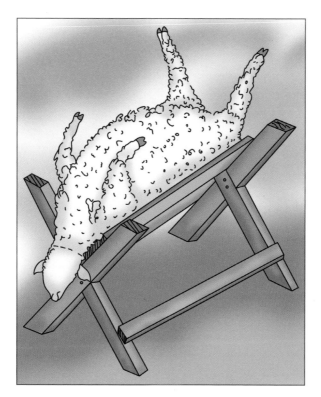

ABOVE: Some may prefer to stun the animal first.

Some prefer to shoot the animal with a .22 in the brain to stun it, then immediately cut its throat. Some simply cut the animal's throat. For those who slaughter more than one occasional animal, a killing and skinning cradle provides the best and most humane means.

The animal is placed in the cradle on its back, and strapped down or held by a second person. The neck is stretched out and downward and the throat immediately cut, cutting completely through the carotid artery, or jugular vein, and just behind the head. Normally the head is removed at this time as well, cutting off at the atlas joint. This is a very quick and humane method of killing as the animal dies almost instantly. This also allows the carcass to completely bleed out quickly as well.

Skinning

Skinning sheep requires a bit more attention to cleanliness. The wool often holds a lot of matter and it's important not to allow dirt or fecal matter to touch the meat. In addition, do not touch the meat with a knife blade or your hands that have contacted the wool. Wool contains dirt and grease that can taint the carcass. Much of the skin is "fisted" off. Use your balled-up fist to "knock" away the skin from the underside, separating it from the fell or membrane covering the meat. Wetting your "fisting" hand makes the chore easier. Always use one hand to hold the skin and wool and one hand to "fist" or hold the knife to cut away the skin.

This is easiest on younger animals, but requires some effort on old animals. You can skin the entire carcass hanging from a gambrel, but many find it easier to skin some portions if the carcass is in a killing and skinning cradle. When skinning lambs or mutton, the wool contains dirt and grease that can taint the meat. Be very careful not to touch the meat with your hand or knife blade that has contacted the wool.

BELOW: With the carcass belly up, encircle each leg with a knife, just through the skin and above the feet. Make an incision down the center of the body and just through the skin. Continue the cut up the inside of each leg. Begin skinning with the legs, down the belly, and along the sides.

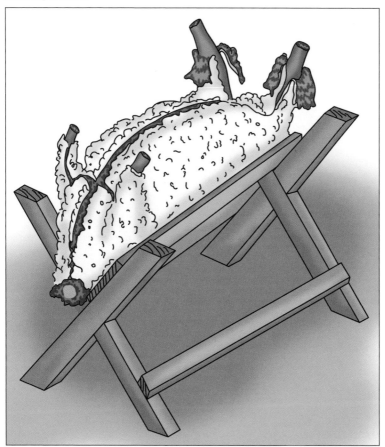

With the carcass in the cradle, make a cut encircling each leg.
Make a cut down the center of the body, from the anus to the neck cut,
making sure you cut from the inside out to prevent contaminating
the meat. Also make sure you do not cut through the muscles of the
abdominal wall, only the skin. Make a cut on the inside of the legs to
meet the centerline body cut. Remove the feet at the joint just above the
hoofs, using a sharp knife and twisting the feet in order to cut through
the cartilage. Cut through the main tendons and back legs to insert a
gambrel. Begin skinning with the legs until you reach the belly and
sides, then fist the hide off down around the sides to the back.

BELOW: Cut off the feet just above the hooves. Make a cut through the breastbone but
not into the intestines. Encircle the anus from the rear, pull it out, and tie off the bung with
a string.

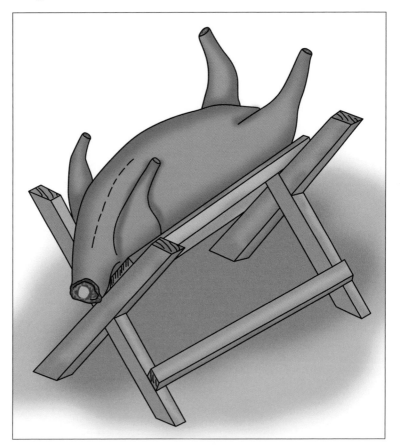

You may wish to start some of the gutting at this point while the carcass is held conveniently in the cradle. Using a saw or large knife, make a cut through the breastbone to separate the rib cage, but do not cut into the intestines. Make a cut encircling the anus, pull out the bung and tie it off. Hoist the carcass and continue skinning out the back and what's left on the sides.

Gutting

With the two initial gutting cuts made, you're ready to finish the job with the carcass hanging. Make a cut through the muscle at the pelvic arch. Continue the cut through the muscle just in front of the pelvic bone, but be very careful not to cut into the intestines. Once you can get your hand in the cut, use your fingers to guide the knife,

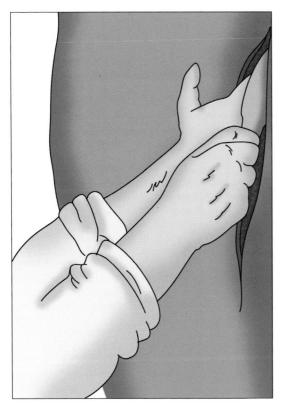

LEFT: Cut behind the large tendons of the back legs, insert a gambrel, and hoist the carcass for the remainder of the job. Using two fingers of one hand and the other to hold the knife, cut through the abdominal wall, being careful not to cut into the paunch.

and cut through the abdominal wall down to the cut made through the breastbone. As you make the cut, the paunch and intestines will fall out. Do not allow them to tear away from the gullet as this can spill contaminating matter.

Reach back to the bung and pull it through the pelvic arch. As you pull down, loosen the attachments inside the carcass. Be careful not to cut into the kidneys. Once the liver is free, cut it loose from the intestines and cut away the gall bladder. Cut away the diaphragm or "skirt" and pull out the heart and lungs, cutting away the attachments to the inside of the carcass. Gently pull the gullet down and out to the throat cut. At this point the entire guts should fall free.

RIGHT: As the intestines and paunch fall out, pull the tied-off bung back through the pelvic arch and cut away interior attachments, including the skirt of the diaphragm. Gently pull the gullet down out the throat and the entire guts will fall free. Remove the heart, kidneys, and tongue from the head, as well as the liver. Cut the gall-bladder from the liver. Wash all in cold, running water and chill.

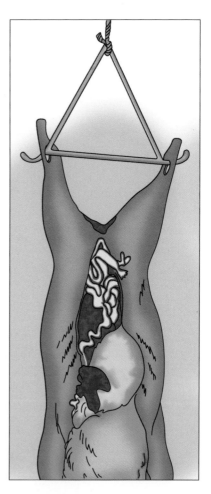

Cut away the delicacies such as the heart and kidneys and remove the tongue. Wash and clean, then chill all the various parts. Thoroughly wash the carcass inside and out, and then place in an area to chill and age. The carcass must be chilled as quickly as possible to below 40°F. The carcass can be cut up after about twenty-four hours, or once it has been chilled properly. The carcass can also be aged if the weather permits. Usually about five to seven days is the normal aging time, but watch for warm temperatures and do not allow the carcass to freeze. Wrapping the carcass with a game bag or clean bed sheet can help prevent the meat from drying out.

Cutting Up

Lamb is often considered an expensive "gourmet" meat due to the prestige cuts such as rib-crown roast, Frenched chops, and rib roast. More common and less expensive cuts include shoulder arm roast, arm roast, shoulder blade roast, and stew meat from the shoulder. Other common cuts include the neck, breast, and foreshank used for stew meat. The rear portion contains the loin, sirloin, and leg.

The leg can be used whole as a roast, bone-in or boneless as a leg of lamb. Or the leg can be cut into a shank half and Frenched lamb leg. All the trimmings can be used as stew meat; as kabob meat, a very popular choice with some cultures; or even as ground meat.

BELOW: Lamb, considered a "gourmet" meat in many cultures, is cut up to produce the prestige cuts such as crown roast and leg of lamb. Lamb or mutton carcasses are normally allowed to hang for five to seven days to age, weather permitting.

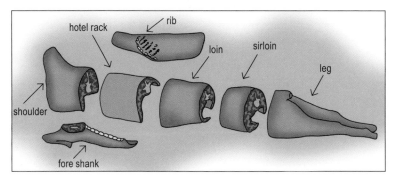

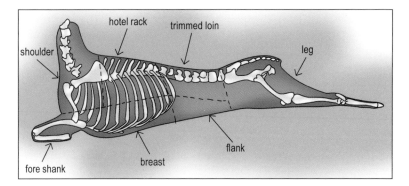

ABOVE: Lay the carcass bone-side up and make the various cuts.

First step is to remove the flank muscles. Separate the fore and hind halves by making a cut through the backbone just behind the ribs. Make a second cut through the entire carcass just in front of the hip bones. This creates the loin section which contains the outside loins and inner tenderloins.

The loin section is cut into lamb chops by first splitting the backbone. Often, however, the cuts are made through the entire carcass, producing double lamb chops.

The remaining hind section contains the sirloin section as well as both legs and shanks. Cut off the sirloin section and cut it into sirloin chops, sirloin roast or rolled double sirloin. Remove the hind shank and debone it for stew meat or ground meat.

Divide the leg into two sections, sawing down the middle of the pelvic arch and the backbone.

Using a saw, make a cut across the front section, through the ribs, to remove a breast and foreshank. The breast can be further cut into riblets, ribs for barbeque, brisket, or rolled or stuffed breast. The foreshank is deboned for stew and ground meat. Make the same cut on the opposite breast, and cut up that section.

Saw down through the backbone and ribs on both sides where the neck vertebrae joins the backbone. This section is often called the rib or hotel rack and contains the chops, crown roasts, and rib roast.

Cut off the neck to create a square shoulder. The shoulder can be further cut into roasts as well as blade chops. The neck can be boned out, or cut into cross sections for bone-in lamb stew, or it can be deboned for stew, kabobs, and ground meat.

Goat

Goat meat, called "chevon," is also a popular and necessary meat in many cultures. Goat breeds include the milking and meat varieties. In the past milk goats were the most popular due to their use for milk, hair, skins, and then meat.

Choosing

Older, nonproductive does (female goats) and male kids, from the milking breed, made up the majority of the meat from goats in the past. Goat meat, however, has become more popular and as a result, the meat breeds are gaining in popularity. Goat meat is also an acquired taste, especially from the older does, but the meat makes good jerky and salami. Goats also don't dress out as efficiently as some other livestock. Goats are slaughtered as kids or adults. Kids may be slaughtered at a very early age or in the case of males, castrated and fed out for five or six months in the same manner as lamb. Very young kids are usually dressed out in the same manner as rabbits, and result in a carcass yielding about 50 percent of the live weight. The carcass is slaughtered in the same manner as rabbits, cutting through the back just in front of the hind legs, and just behind the front legs. The saddle or center section is cut in half and the legs cut apart to produce six pieces of meat. A goat that has been fed out will produce a carcass from 30 to 50 percent of the live weight.

Killing

Feed must be withheld for twelve hours prior to slaughter, but provide plenty of water. The animal must be restrained, and then killed by stunning with a sharp blow to the skull, or with a gunshot to the brain. Goats are somewhat more difficult to kill, because they just seem more "cagey." Some suggest making the shot from the back of the head so the animal doesn't see you and become frightened. Immediately cut through the jugular vein, just under the jaw and hang the animal head down to allow the blood to thoroughly drain. Some like to also immediately remove the head by continuing the throat cut around the neck at the atlas joint and twisting off the head.

Skinning

Make a cut from between the hind legs to the throat cut, making sure you cut only through the skin and not into the abdominal muscle. Cut along the inside of each leg to the centerline cut and encircle the legs at the ankle joint. Make a deep cut around the anus, pull out the bung and tie it off with a string to prevent contamination with fecal matter. Push the bung and colon back into the body cavity. Cut off the skin at the base of the tail and then skin out the animal, fisting off and peeling the hide, alternating with the skinning knife as needed.

BELOW: Goat meat, especially that from meat-breed goats, is also extremely popular. Goat meat may consist of very young kids or those fed out to five or six months. Goats are killed and cut up in much the same manner as for lamb and mutton.

Gutting

Once you've removed the skin, make a cut from the pelvic arch to the point of the breastbone, cutting only through the abdominal muscles. This will allow the stomach and intestines to roll out. Pull the bung and colon down and out. Very carefully remove the bladder, making sure you don't cut it. Remove the liver, and carefully cut away the gallbladder. Wash the liver in cold water and chill immediately. Cut through the gullet to further free the stomach and intestines. Saw the brisket to open the area and pull out the heart and lungs, cutting the skirt or diaphragm to allow them to come out. Wash the carcass thoroughly inside and out with cold water and wipe dry.

Cutting Up

Goat carcasses are usually cut up in the same manner as lamb, and often used in many of the same recipes. Or you can bone out the meat in the same manner as venison. Goat meat, however, has less fat than lamb and tends to be leaner. Goat meat dries out quicker and will also freezer burn quicker. Make sure goat meat is thoroughly wrapped and packaged and don't store it overly long in your freezer. Trimmings from goat meat can also be made into sausage, but must be mixed with pork.

Rabbits

Rabbits are easy to raise, easy to slaughter, and provide great and healthful meat. Rabbit meat is a staple in many countries. The meat is fine-grained, semi-red, and extremely tasty. Some say it tastes like chicken, but it has its own flavor, although it's often prepared in the same manner as chicken.

Choosing

As with other livestock, animals of any age can be butchered, although the younger animals are the most tender and have the most

ABOVE: Domestic rabbits offer another very healthy meat and are easy to raise and butcher.

delicate flavor. Young rabbits, from two to six months in age are called fryers because they make great fried rabbit in the same manner as chicken fryers. Older animals can also be butchered, but the meat is best in stews.

Killing

Feed must be withheld for twelve hours prior to slaughter, but provide plenty of water. Due to the chance of tularemia, wear rubber

BELOW: Rabbits are commonly killed by rapping behind the ears with a sturdy club. Then cut off the head.

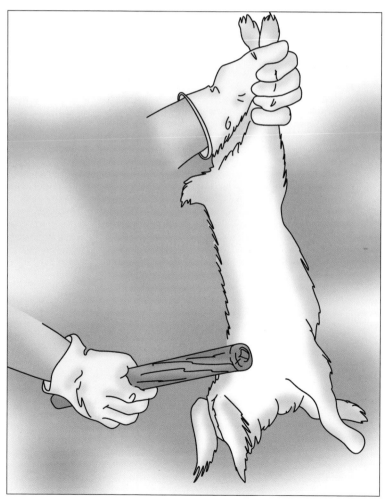

gloves while butchering rabbits. The most common method to kill a rabbit is to hold it by the hind legs and strike it sharply across the back of the neck and behind the ears, with a sturdy club. Once the animal is stunned, immediately cut its throat. Then remove the head, cutting through the skin, meat and twisting off at the atlas joint.

Skinning

Make a cut to separate a tendon in one hind leg and suspend the carcass from a wire or gambrel. Cut off the other feet using heavy-duty kitchen shears or pruning shears.

BELOW: Rabbits are also easy to skin. Hang by one foot from a wire hook. Make an incision down the groin and on the inside of each leg and peel the skin off.

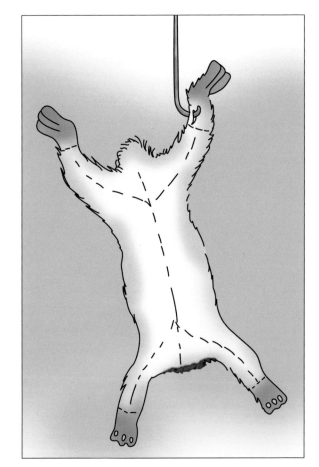

Make a cut encircling the hock of the suspended leg, then continue the cut down to the groin. Make a cut on the opposite hind leg in the same manner. Peel off the skin from the back legs and cut off the tail. The remainder of the rabbit skin is very easy to remove, simply peeling off the entire carcass like a glove. There is one problem, however: rabbit fur tends to stick to the carcass, so avoid cutting through the hair and try to keep as much fur from contacting the carcass as possible. Another method, and one used by my granddad, was to make a slit through the skin across the center of the back, grasp the skin on each side of the slit and pull with both hands to pull the skin off both the front and rear of the animal. Then cut the feet and head free.

Gutting

Make a shallow cut along the centerline of the belly from the groin and through the rib cage, being careful not to cut into the intestines.

RIGHT: Make a shallow cut down the centerline of the belly, encircle the anus, and pull the entire intestines out.

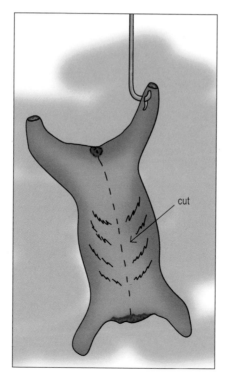

cut

Cut around the anus and the entire offal is easily removed. Experienced rabbit dressers simply give a flick of their wrist and snap out the offal. Save the heart, kidneys and liver, carefully cutting the gall bladder from the liver. Place all in ice water to chill. Thoroughly wash the carcass in cold water.

Cutting Up

Traditionally rabbit is cut into six pieces. Make one cut behind the shoulders and one cut in front of the back legs to produce the "saddle." Cut the saddle in half lengthwise and divide the shoulders and back legs into two pieces each. Wash the meat, and then chill as rapidly as possible. Do not allow the meat to sit overnight in ice water as it causes the meat to fade to a milky white, mottled appearance. Chill the meat dry, but covered, in the refrigerator.

RIGHT: Rabbit is commonly cut into six pieces: two front legs, two back legs, and two saddle pieces. Or, on larger rabbits, cut two back legs, two front legs, a saddle piece, and two belly pieces.

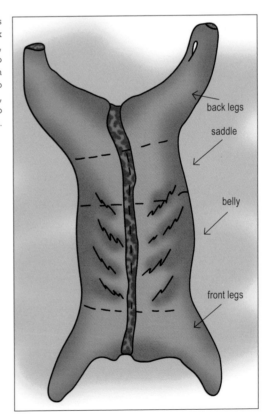

back legs

saddle

belly

front legs

⑦
Venison and Other Wild Game

MANY HUNTERS DO not raise or butcher domestic animals, but instead hunt venison and other big game, and by necessity butcher and field dress the animal. I often wonder about hunters who don't do the complete process. Butchering a deer is a relatively easy process, and with my complete boning method, requires little in the way of tools or skill.

The main advantage of doing it yourself, however, is meat quality. When you take your deer to a slaughter plant you may or may not get back ground meat from only your deer. Some plants cut up carcasses and then grind meat in large lots instead of grinding the individual carcasses separately. Even if you've been extremely careful not to contaminate your meat while field dressing, perhaps another hunter wasn't as careful.

Small game and wild fowl are also pursued by many hunters. Squirrels, rabbits, upland game such as doves, quail and pheasant, as well as wild turkeys, ducks, and geese all provide excellent table fare. Unlike their domestic cousins, small game and birds are more lean, yet high in protein. Dressing small game and birds properly is extremely easy and they should be done as quickly as possible, especially in hot weather to prevent spoilage.

Fish have also been a staple food of mankind from the beginning. Proper care after the catch and proper dressing can make a big difference in the quality of the meat. Again, the most important factor is keeping the fish fresh or quickly cooled down after the catch.

Wild game meat offers some health advantages. Following is a chart showing the benefits.

THE SKINNY ON GAME MEAT

Type of Meat	Fat	Saturated Fat	Calories	Protein
Deer	3.2g	1.2g	158	30.2g
Elk	1.9g	0.7g	146	30.2g
Antelope	2.7g	1.0g	150	29.4g
Lean Roast Beef	14.3g	5.7g	249	27.0g
Lean Ham	5.8g	1.9g	153	24.8g
Salmon	5.8g	1.4g	163	24.5g
Chicken Breast*	3.5g	1.1g	163	31.5g

SOURCE: U.S. Department of Agriculture (for 3.5-ounce portions)   *roasted, no skin

Venison

Choosing

Wild game meat, such as deer, elk, or moose, is some of the best red meat you can eat. First, it's leaner; actually it's a natural "grass-fed" meat, although deer tend to eat more of a variety of plants than just grass. Venison has about 2 percent fat, compared to beef with 30 percent fat. Just like with home-grown meat, selecting a wild game animal for food is also important.

Younger animals are naturally tender, and females are usually less tough and have less gamey flavor than male animals. An old

ABOVE: Wild game, especially venison, is one of the healthiest meats. It's lean, with about 2 percent fat, compared to beef with 30 percent fat.

trophy buck, during the height of the rut, can be both tough and gamey. Old bulls are usually ground up into hamburger and old bucks should be as well. If you're trophy hunting, you'll be stuck with an older, tougher animal.

Just as with butchering domestic livestock, stressed animals produce lower-quality meat. A deer or other wild game that is hit poorly and runs a distance also has the chance of "fiery meat" due to the release of the same adrenaline and lactic acid as in domestic animals. Regardless of gun or bow, it's important to strike the vitals for a clean, quick kill. This is not always possible, but it's important to practice with your gun or bow and be proficient.

As with domestic livestock, younger animals are the best choice for tenderness and have a less "gamey flavor."

Then take only shots that will ensure a good kill. I don't take running shots because running deer are usually scared or running for a reason. Even if you do make a clean kill, which is rare, the meat may have an off taste.

Several years ago a friend and I were quail hunting on my property when my bird dog jumped a buck from a brush pile fairly near a major highway. The buck jumped out, lunged forward onto his front legs, which were both broken, tried to lunge again, falling over. My setter grabbed him by the tail and the battle began. I finally killed the buck with a knife, cutting his throat. Apparently the buck had been hit by an automobile on the highway alongside my property and had hidden in the brush pile for days. I called the Conservation Agent and explained the situation. "Go ahead and dress him and keep him," he replied. I did, but the meat wasn't fit to eat, almost powder dry and very strong tasting.

Many people find venison too gamey for their taste. Killed,

LEFT: It's important to make a good killing shot, with a quick death for quality meat.

field dressed, and processed wrong, venison can indeed be strong flavored. Venison has been a major meat source in our household for decades. We've learned to cook it in many different ways. Our guests often don't know they're eating venison as they comment on the great-tasting food. Venison, like beef, benefits from aging.

Aging creates more tenderness, but also requires consistently cool temperatures (staying below 40°F) for the length of the aging time. The carcass must also be quickly chilled down to 40°F before the aging period. The carcass is typically aged by hanging in a cool area with plenty of circulation and safe from pests such as cats, dogs, even coyotes. The carcass can be hung skinned or unskinned. Skinned carcasses will cool quicker. The carcass will form a hard, dry "skin" on the outside or "fell," the membrane covering the meat and keeping the meat moist. You can also cover the carcass with a cheese-cloth game bag to provide some protection. Make sure the animal is properly field dressed and washed, and the body cavity propped open to get good air circulation. We typically hang deer for seven to ten days, but it depends mostly on the temperature at the time. If you don't have consistently cold weather, or the weather alternates between freezing and too warm, add the freezing time to the aging time. In hot climates hanging to age is not an option. The carcass can be quartered and placed in an old refrigerator to age. As there is no air circulation, you'll need to move the pieces around frequently to prevent blood pooling in one area. If possible, stand the pieces on end so they will drain properly.

Field Dressing

Proper field dressing is a major step in safe, quality venison. It's extremely important to field dress as quickly as possible after the animal has been killed to allow body heat to dissipate rapidly.

RIGHT: Venison is often hung to age, depending on the weather and ambient temperature, and then cut up.

Venison can also be heavily contaminated with fecal bacteria—the degree varying with the hunter's skill, location of the wound, and other factors. Take all necessary steps to avoid puncturing the digestive tract, a very common problem.

Always have the necessary tools for field dressing readily available. In addition to a good skinning knife, you'll need a twelve-inch piece of sturdy string, a plastic bag for holding the liver and heart, and rubber or plastic gloves. Although the standard food-safe rubber gloves can be used, a better choice is "vet" gloves found at farm supply stores. These long plastic gloves come up to your elbows. This prevents getting blood and other matter on your hunting clothes, a common problem when you're reaching into a bloody carcass. These

BELOW: Proper field dressing is the first key in safe and quality game meat. Do so as soon as possible after the kill.

gloves can be carried in a plastic food bag in a pocket or in your hunting pack. My nephew Morgan also carries a small container of wet-wipes in his hunting pack. A drag harness or section of sturdy rope that can be fashioned into a drag is also handy.

Sticking or cutting the throat is not necessary and can contaminate the meat. Do not cut off the scent glands located on the hocks. This also isn't necessary and contaminates the knife blade and then the meat. Do tag the animal with the necessary game tag before proceeding to field dress. As with all types of butchering, the field dressing can be done in a number of ways. Following is the method I've used successfully for many years. Under the right circumstances I can field dress a deer in about three minutes.

BELOW: Roll the animal onto its back and prop in place or hold with your legs. Make a cut between the legs and down to the pelvic arch bone. Then continue the cut through the pelvic arch, being careful not to cut into the paunch or bladder.

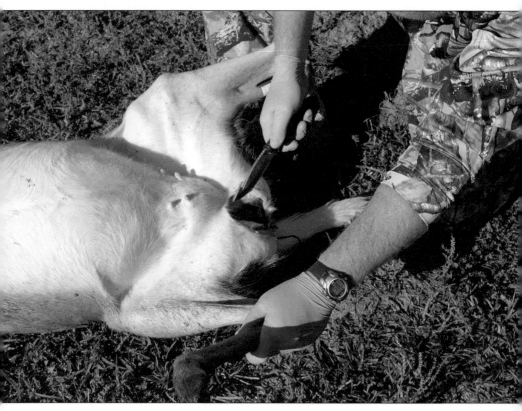

The first step is to roll the animal onto its back on a flat spot. Sometimes that takes a bit of dragging here in the Ozarks where I live. You may even have to prop up the body with sticks or stones. Prop the head just a bit higher than the rest of the body. Straddle the animal facing toward the head. On small deer I place my legs inside their back legs to force the legs outwards and help hold the body in position. On bigger animals, I use one of my legs to force one of their back legs into an upright position. A buddy can be a great help in field dressing, especially by holding the animal in place. Check your local laws regarding leaving the genitals on the carcass. Some states require the genitals to remain on the field-dressed deer until the deer has been through a check station. Many states, these days,

BELOW: Cut around the bung, or anus, from the rear of the animal. Pull out the bung and tie it off with a string.

however, use electronic checking and this is not necessary. If a buck, and allowed by law, cut away the penis and scrotum, slicing to one side just through the skin, then peeling out and slicing the opposite side. Do not remove, but allow them to hang back over the anus. If a doe is still lactating and the udder is full, cut away and remove the udder, but do not cut into it. If the milk from the udder contacts the meat, it can create a strong taste. Make a cut with the knife held fairly flat through the skin and muscle between the legs and down to the pelvic arch. Be careful not to cut into the paunch at the beginning of the cut. Locate the white line in the center of the pelvic arch and cut on it through the pelvic bone. On smaller deer you can do this with a sturdy skinning knife; on larger animals a game saw or hatchet is necessary. Push down on the inside of the haunches to further spread the pelvic bone apart.

From the rear of the animal, cut around the bung on the sides and back. Pull the bung out and tie it off with a string. This prevents getting fecal matter on the carcass through the remainder of the process. Or, you may prefer to cut around the bung and pull it out first before splitting the pelvic bone. Hunter's Specialties makes a great tool for this chore, the Butt Out. In this case the bung is pulled out as the first step.

Simply insert the Butt Out into the anal canal, making sure the handle is flush against the canal. Twist the handle until you feel the tool grab the membrane and then twist one half turn more. Steadily pull the Butt Out from the anal canal. This will pull out the canal membrane. Extract about ten to twelve inches of the membrane, and tie it off.

The next step is opening the paunch and can be the hardest part. However, if you have a skinning knife with a gut hook, this step is actually very easy. Starting at the point of the breastbone, make a small incision just through the skin and muscle, but not into the intestines.

ABOVE: The Hunter's Specialties Butt Out makes this chore quick and easy. Insert the Butt Out, then pull out the bung and tie it off.

BELOW: Using a knife with a gut hook, start an incision through the skin and muscles at the point of the breastbone and cut down to the pelvic cut.

Insert the gut hook in the cut and pull down, slicing through the skin and muscle. The gut hook prevents cutting into the paunch.

The paunch will steadily rise up and out of the animal as you make the cut. Continue the cut to join with the cut through the pelvic arch. There will be a fairly heavy muscle just ahead of the pelvic arch. Cut through this with the knife blade, again being careful not to cut into the intestines or the bladder, which lies just below the arch.

Turn the knife around and make a cut from the tip of the breastbone through the center of the ribs up to the throat. This can be done fairly easily on a small animal. On larger animals you may need to cut through the skin with a knife, and then complete the cut with a meat

BELOW: Or make the cut with a knife blade, pointing outward and up, using your fingers to push the paunch and intestines down and away from the cut. Be careful not to cut into the paunch.

saw. If you're dressing a trophy buck, do not cut high on the throat: just to the front point of the chest, in order to save the cape.

Reach up into the chest cavity and cut the gullet attachments. Pull the heart, liver, and other intestines from the cavity, cutting the skirt or diaphragm membrane as necessary. Be extremely careful not to cut into the tenderloins located just inside the backbone.

Roll the carcass over on its side and the entire intestines will fall out. Pull the penis and bung back through the pelvic opening and pull the intestines away from the carcass, cutting away interior attachments as necessary.

Lift up on the head of the animal to allow blood that has collected in the cavity to drain out. If fresh, clean water is available, thoroughly wash the inside of the carcass.

BELOW: Turn the knife around and cut through the breastbone toward the throat. On larger animals you may need a saw or hand hatchet to cut the bone.

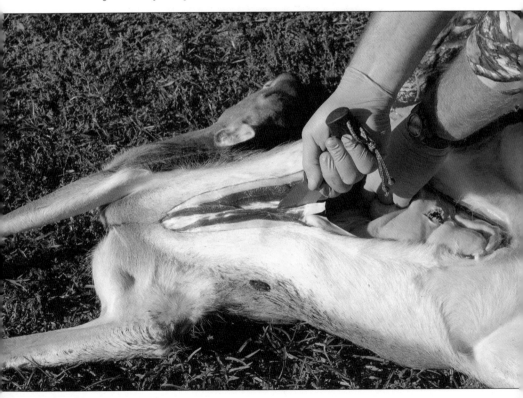

ABOVE: Reach into the chest cavity and cut the gullet and windpipe.

BELOW: Pull the intestines, heart, and liver through the openings, cutting the skirt or diaphragm to release the heart and lungs.

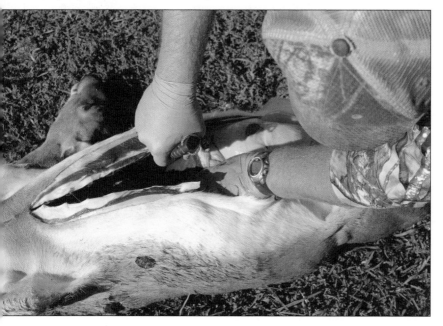

Cut the liver away from the intestines, and cut away the gallbladder, cutting off a bit of liver with the gallbladder attached. Remove the heart. Place the liver and heart in a plastic bag. You're now ready to transport the animal. Keep the opening of the body cavity clean during transport.

Processing

Deer, as well as elk and moose, can be processed in any number of ways. Moose and elk are normally processed in much the same manner as a beef. Deer are often processed in a variety of ways. Deer can be skinned, then cut up in the same basic method as for other domestic livestock, following the same basic cuts. Or, deer can be

BELOW: Roll the carcass over on its side and the intestines will fall out. Turn the carcass over on its belly to allow blood to drain out. If possible wash the interior with fresh, cold water.

partially processed in that manner and other portions boned out. Or you can bone out the entire carcass, my favorite method. I'll describe the latter two and you can make your own choices.

Skinning

If you're processing in the traditional manner, the first step is skinning out the carcass. Depending on the weather and the time I have available during hunting season (sometimes I have a half dozen or more deer to do), I'll skin before hanging and aging, or after. If the weather is ideal, I prefer to skin before hanging and aging and as soon as possible after the animal has been killed. The skin comes off

BELOW: Field deer are often field dressed and quartered at the same time in the field, for easier transporting.

easier while still fresh. If I'm skinning in the traditional manner, the first step is to saw off the rear legs below the hocks and the front legs in front of the knees. There is almost no meat on the legs of a deer. The main problem with skinning a deer is the brittle hair, which comes out easily and also cuts and breaks easily, with the result being hair on the meat. The method described results in the least amount of hair on the meat, although you'll always have some. Make all cuts from the underside of the skin and outward to avoid cutting hair as much as possible.

A cut is made in each hind leg between the hock and main tendon to insert a gambrel. The deer is then hoisted, head down, and high enough that I can easily reach the chest and front legs. Slide a skinning knife under the skin on the inside of a front leg and make a cut on the inside of the leg, continuing to the field-dressing cut on the throat. Then skin out the front leg around to the shoulder. Repeat this for the opposite leg. Many people start at the rear and skin downward, but the hide falls down over the shoulder and front legs, making it harder to skin them. Once both front legs and shoulders have been

BELOW: To skin in the traditional manner saw off the feet, make a cut behind the rear-left tendons and insert a gambrel.

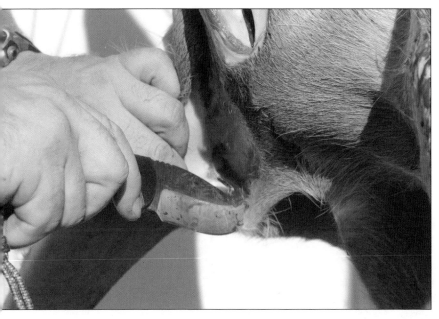

ABOVE: Hoist the carcass head down and make an incision in the inner skin of the front legs to the neck. Always cut from the underside of the skin to avoid getting hairs on the meat.

BELOW: Skin out the front legs.

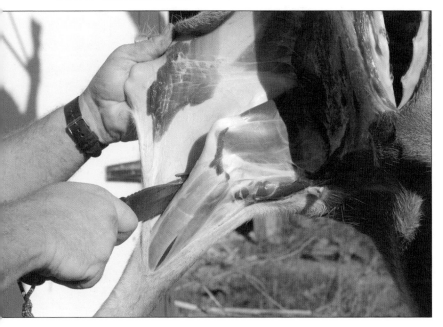

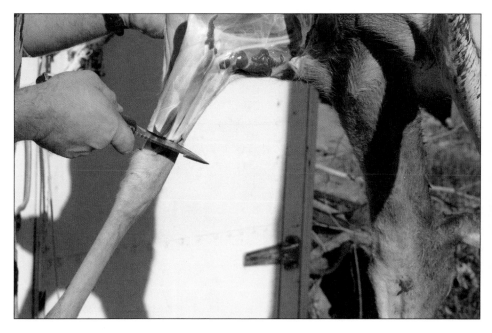

ABOVE: Make a cut encircling the skin of the front legs.

BELOW: Skin out the hind legs, starting with a cut made from the inside of the skin on the inside of the hams.

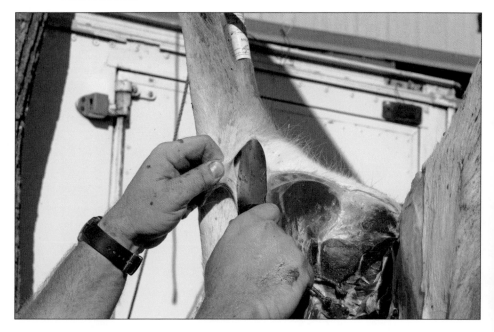

ABOVE: Grasp the flap of skin and pull back over the hams, using a knife to help cut away from the fell, or membrane, covering the muscles.

skinned out, lower the carcass until you can easily reach the hind legs, but do not let the front of the carcass touch the ground. Slide the skinning knife blade in under the skin on the inside of the hams, from the initial field-dressing cut. Turn the blade sharp edge out and slice through the skin up to the cut made to remove the hind legs. Grasp the flap of skin on the inside, next to the pelvic arch, and peel it up over and toward the ham, using the edge of the skinning knife to help release the skin from the membrane covering the muscle. Continue this process until you reach the back of the ham.

This is actually the hardest part of the skinning process as the skin sticks to the meat on the top of the ham. Grasp the skin on the outside edge of the ham and peel and slice it off until you reach the carcass side. Finish skinning out the back leg and repeat for the opposite leg. When you reach the tail, cut it off. With the tail free, as well as the skin from each leg, you can often peel the majority of the skin free. Grasp the hanging skin or tail and pull down. If the carcass

ABOVE: Encircle the skin of the back legs.

BELOW: Skin over the back of the hams and cut off the tail.

You can usually peel the skin
off the back and sides, using
a knife only when necessary
to help loosen the skin.

Continue skinning down to the head.

is still fresh, the skin will often simply pull down almost to the shoulders. The skin will still stick in some places, mostly on the flanks and brisket. Use the knife with a sweeping, slicing motion to cut the skin away as needed. Be careful not to cut into the skin from the underside as you again risk getting hair on the meat. Be extra careful if you're saving the hide or the animal is a trophy buck.

Continue skinning down around the shoulders and the neck until you reach the head. Remove the head at the atlas joint by cutting through the meat with a knife, then twisting off the head. If you have

BELOW: Remove the head at the atlas joint, twisting as needed and cutting through the tendons with a knife.

meat that has been possibly contaminated by fecal matter or shot area, cut it off, then wash the knife with disinfectant.

Cutting Up

Before you begin cutting up the carcass, have everything you need on hand. This includes a clean work surface, pans for ground-meat pieces, and a pail or other container to contain the discarded pieces, and paper towels to wipe your knife blade of hair.

You can divide the carcass into quarters in much the same manner as a beef or pork, producing two halves with two forequarters and two hindquarters. This results in loin chops, steaks, and ribs. A more traditional venison division is often used.

Begin the processing with the carcass still hanging by its hind legs, but do not split the carcass. The first step is to remove the front shoulders. The front shoulders come off easily. Grasping a front leg, pull the shoulder out and away from the rib cage. You'll see a division between the two. Using a long, boning-style butcher knife, slice between the two. Pull the shoulder upward as you slice and you'll see the cartilage move on the top of the shoulder. Continue cutting between the shoulder and rib cage around the shoulder cartilage and it will come free easily.

Make sure the shoulder you're holding is secure when it comes free. The shoulder produces the traditional roasts and ground meat,

BELOW: The carcass can be cut up in the same manner as beef but is traditionally cut into somewhat different cuts.

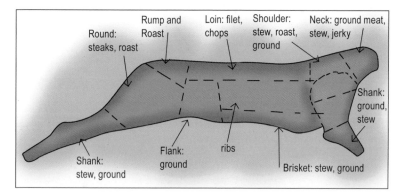

Round: steaks, roast — Rump and Roast — Loin: filet, chops — Shoulder: stew, roast, ground — Neck: ground meat, stew, jerky — Shank: ground, stew — Shank: stew, ground — Flank: ground — ribs — Brisket: stew, ground

ABOVE: With the carcass hanging head down, grasp a front leg and pull it out and away from the body. Then, using a long boning knife, cut between the leg and body to remove the front shoulder. Lay aside and repeat with the opposite shoulder.

while the shank portion produces meat for stews, soups, and ground meat.

The second step is to remove the loins from the backbone. Again a boning-style knife is the best choice. Make a cut down each side of the backbone as close to the backbone and as deep as possible. Then insert the knife against the ribs and, starting at the top of the loin, slice along the outside of the ribs and to the backbone, meeting the first cut. Cut down to the end of the hanging front quarter. This produces a deer loin about eighteen to twenty-four inches long and two inches thick. Hold the meat strip with one hand as you cut it free with the opposite. This tender portion of the deer makes great steaks and

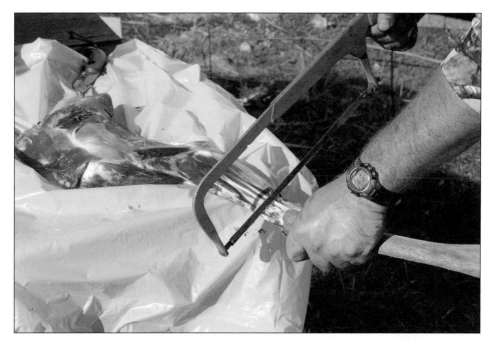

ABOVE: Saw off the front legs.

BELOW: The shoulders can be cut into roasts or ground meat. The shanks can be used for ground meat or stew meat.

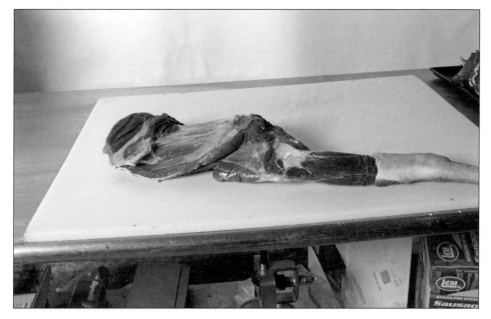

roasts and is fantastic smoked. Repeat these steps for the opposite loin. Inside the carcass on either side of the backbone are the two tenderloins. Using a boning knife, peel them out. These are the most

BELOW: Quite often the loins are boned out. Make a cut following the rib cage.

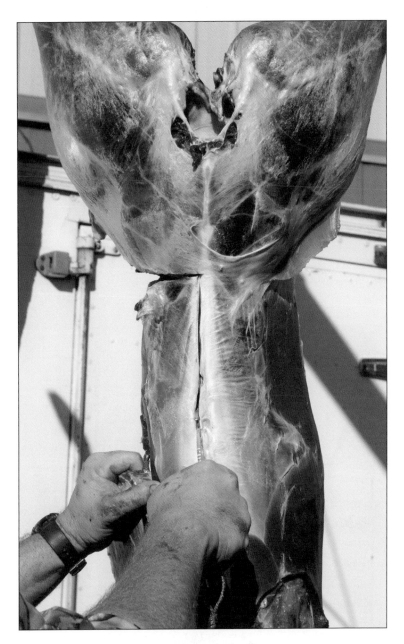

ABOVE: Then make a cut along the side of the backbone.

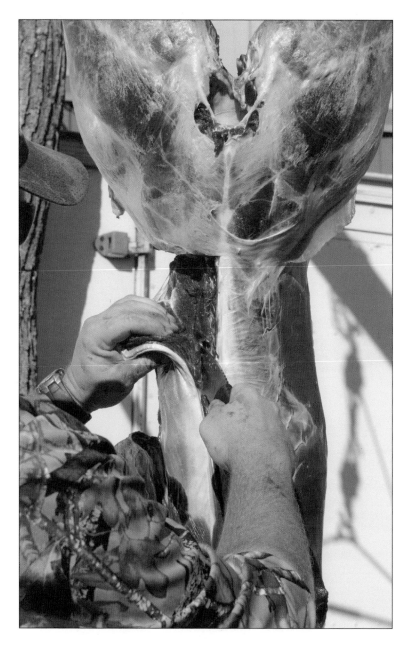

ABOVE: Peel out the loin.

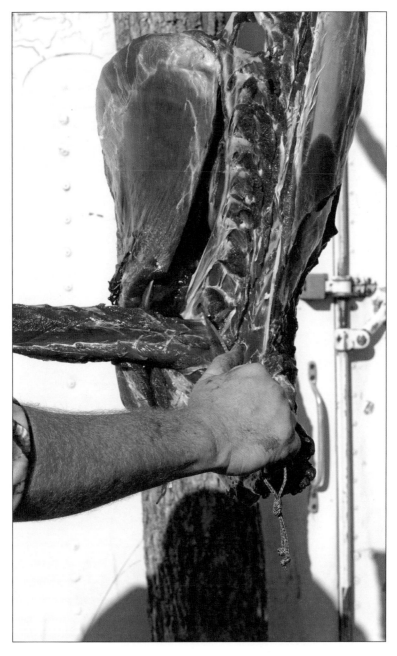

ABOVE: Finish cutting off the loin and then repeat for the opposite side.

ABOVE: Peel the back fat away from the loin, using a boning knife to start the cut, then pull away with your hands. The loins can be left whole for smoking or cut into steaks for grilling.

tender portions of the deer carcass. They make great "steak" hors d'oeuvres for the grill.

The third step is to remove the hindquarters from the front quarter or rib cage. Cut the hindquarter off at the joint, starting the cut through the flank, making the cut on both sides to the backbone.

Cut through the backbone with a meat saw. Again be careful to not drop the front rib sections.

On a large deer you may want help in holding the front sections while making the cut, or slide a table or other support under the carcass. The hindquarters produce rump roasts, roasts, or round steaks. The shank produces soup bones, stew, and ground meat. Remove the hindquarters from the gambrel and place on a sturdy worktable. Saw down the center of the backbone to produce two hindquarters. Then bone out the meat, using a sharp boning-style knife. Simply

ABOVE: Saw the backbone and rib cage away from the hindquarters.

cut around the bones to remove them, following the natural division lines of the muscles. Then cut into steaks or roasts as desired. The steaks will be round steaks as they are cut from the "round" of the hindquarter. You can also use a meat saw to saw the hindquarters into more traditional steaks.

The remaining carcass contains the ribs and neck. Lay the carcass on a table and saw off the front shoulder portion still left on the carcass. This can be made into a shoulder roast or used as ground meat. The neck is cut off and the meat used for stews, soup, or ground meat. Saw the ribs from the backbone, and then saw into three- to four-inch-wide strips.

Complete Boning Out

The third method is completely boning out the carcass. This is definitely our favorite venison dressing method. No bones are cut through. Not only do you avoid any possible health problems with

ABOVE: Remove the backbone from the rib cage and saw the rib cage into rib pieces. Or bone out the entire rib cage.

BELOW: Take down the hindquarters and lay on a sturdy table. Cut into the traditional steaks and roasts or bone out the meat.

CWD, but you end up with no bones to take up space in your freezer, and you don't even need a meat saw. You'll end up with lots of boneless loin, steaks, roasts, and ground meat. In this method the deer is normally skinned and boned at the same time, so the skin is left on during the aging process until you're ready to cut up the carcass.

If using this method with a young deer or antlerless deer, the head is even left on the boned-out carcass. Or, you can skin the animal in the normal manner, remove the head if a trophy buck, allow the carcass to age the desired amount of time, and then bone it out. I call this method one-step deer processing.

When using one-step deer processing, the legs are not sawed off before skinning. The deer is hoisted so you can easily reach the front legs and the legs are encircled with a cut just behind the knees, then a cut made on the inside of each front leg from the encircling cut to the throat cut made during field dressing. The front legs are then skinned out to the shoulders.

The carcass is lowered so you can easily reach the rear legs. Encircle the rear legs, make a cut from the ham field-dressing cut to

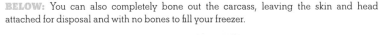

BELOW: You can also completely bone out the carcass, leaving the skin and head attached for disposal and with no bones to fill your freezer.

the encircling cut and skin the hind legs down to the hams, then skin down the hams. When you reach the tail, you can either cut it off or skin it out. Either is fairly easily done. If you're saving the skin, peel out the tail.

Continue peeling and skinning down to the head. You can remove the head with the skin attached and leave the carcass to age, or continue the process. If the latter, merely allow the skin to hang down over the head and begin the boning process. Remove the front shoulders in the same manner as before, slicing between them and the rib cage. Lay them aside to be deboned later.

Remove the flanks. These have little meat, and are often bloody from the killing shot, but some meat can usually be salvaged. Cut away any bloody meat. The flank pieces are often used in ground meat or stews. Remove the loins by cutting between the backbone and ribs on the sides, beginning at the juncture or where the hindquarter ends at the backbone. Cut down toward the neck until you can peel out the loin pieces. Remove the tenderloins inside the carcass and against the backbone.

While the carcass is still hanging, lower it so you can reach the hindquarters easily and debone the meat from the hindquarters. This is fairly easy to do, if you follow the muscle joints, cutting around the bones with a boning knife as necessary.

Debone the neck. My nephew, Morgan, even likes to get the meat between each rib for his ground jerky. The final step is to debone the front shoulders. All that's left is the deboned carcass and skin.

Clean all pieces of meat to remove any hair. Cut away any bloody or excessively fatty areas, or those with gristle or excess sinew. The latter is a common problem with venison and other wild game.

Ground Meat

We usually put all the boned meat into the ground-meat pot, except for the loins and tenderloins. These are saved for the grill or smoker. We also usually save one hindquarter to cut into round steaks for baked steak, Swiss steak, and stroganoff.

ABOVE: The resulting boned-out carcass with skin ready for disposal.

ABOVE: Venison makes great ground meat for chili, tacos, and summer sausage. Make sure you trim off all fat and sinew.

We eat a lot of ground venison in chili, tacos, taco salads, and summer sausage. For more on making your own summer sausage, see *The Complete Guide to Sausage Making*. We also make a lot of deer jerky from the ground meat. For more on making your own deer jerky see my book, *The Complete Jerky Book*.

Deer meat fat quickly becomes rancid, so cut all possible fat, sinew, and gristle from the meat to be ground. Then cut the meat into chunks or strips that will go through your meat grinder. Wear food-safe gloves at all times while working up and grinding deer meat.

Getting Rid of Gamey Flavors

Some people don't like the taste of venison, and indeed some venison meat can be quite strong. An overnight marinade can be used to help cut some of the gamey flavor. Some like to marinade roasts and steaks in milk. One simple marinade is soy sauce and lemon pepper. Or you can use commercial marinades. We like teriyaki marinade on our grilled loin steaks.

Big Game

In addition to whitetail deer, other North American big game includes mule deer, antelope, the various bighorn sheep, mountain goats, bear, buffalo, elk, moose, caribou, javelina, and wild hog. The method of field dressing and butchering depends on the game species, the size of the game, and the location where killed. Regardless, the animal must be field dressed as quickly as possible. Smaller animals, such as antelope and small mule deer, can be field dressed in much the same manner as for whitetails. If antelope hunting in hot weather, quickly skin, gut, and quarter the carcass; then place the quarters in a cooler. If this is not possible, hang in the shade and cover with a cheesecloth game bag.

Bigger game, including elk, moose, buffalo, sheep, and goats, require a somewhat different approach due to their size and/or location of the kill. Again, the first step is to immediately field dress. A couple of sections of rope and a come-along can be used to help hold the legs up and apart for this step. You'll also need a sturdy knife and a packable game saw.

You can skin and then quarter the animal, or usually in the case of backpacking and horsepacking, leave the skin on until you get to camp, where the sections can then be skinned and placed in cheesecloth bags, and then into packbags for packing out. If you prefer to skin out the carcass and a handy and sturdy tree limb is available, you can partially hoist the carcass for skinning. Or leave the carcass on the ground—skin one side, roll the carcass over, and skin the opposite.

The carcass is then cut into quarters for easier transporting— whether on your back, horseback, by boat, plane, or other means. With this method you can reduce an elk to more manageable pieces between 65 and 130 pounds each. You can even cut larger animals into six or seven sections. If allowed, boning out the meat can reduce the weight even more. Make sure you understand the game laws in the state the animal is taken, regarding transportation of game meat.

LEFT: Big game, especially the larger species often require a somewhat different approach to field dressing, especially those taken in the mountains and back country.

RIGHT: You'll need a sturdy all-purpose knife and a packable meat saw for big game, plus plastic bags, gloves and plenty of light-weight rope.

Quite often you'll have to pack the carcass out on your back or by horse.

There are several different methods of quartering. The first is to simply cut into four quarters. Bend a front leg and cut through the skin at the joint. Use a knife and saw to remove the lower leg. Repeat for the opposite front leg. Some like to remove the lower portion of the back legs as well, especially if backpacking. Some feel, however, that leaving them in place makes it easier to secure the back legs to a pack or pack frame, but they do tend to catch on tree limbs and brush.

Skin the neck and saw off the head. If the animal is a trophy, after field dressing skin out the cape, taking care to leave plenty of skin in place. If not a trophy, it's still best to skin out the neck area. Cut off the head with the cape attached.

Spread the carcass as much as possible and cutting from the inside to help prevent getting hair on the meat, make a cut between the third and fourth ribs on each side to the backbone. Using a saw cut through the backbone and complete the cut through the skin.

Make a cut through the skin, down the center of the backbone on the front half and peel the skin away on either side of the cut. Prop the half in place and saw through the backbone. Repeat for the rear half and you have four quarters ready to transport.

If you need smaller sections, say of a moose, it can be cut into six sections. After removing the head and lower legs, saw down the

BELOW: After field dressing, first step is to remove the lower legs. Use a sharp knife or a meat saw to cut through tendons.

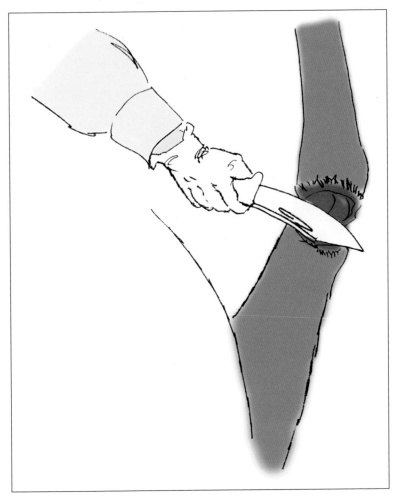

middle of the backbone to create two halves. Then cut just behind the front leg and just in front of the rear leg on each side. You can also cut off the neck creating seven pieces.

Several years ago a horse-packing guide showed me an alternative method of packing out elk quarters. It's quick and easy and doesn't require a packsaddle. Quarter in the same manner as before, but do not cut through the skin on the spine, leaving the quarters attached at the spine by the skin. The entire half can be placed on a horse, skin side down and the legs of the carcass tied with a strap running under the horse's belly.

Wild hogs and javelinas are usually field dressed and skinned in the same manner as described in the earlier chapter on pork. Wild hogs can carry diseases, make sure you wear protective gloves while

BELOW: Cape the animal for a mount, or cut around the skin where the neck joins the head and cut off the head.

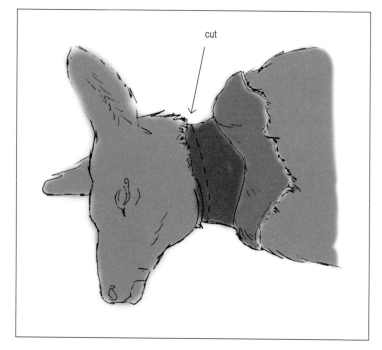

BELOW: Spread the carcass and working from the inside, cut between the third and fourth ribs on both sides, cut through the skin as well. Then saw through the ribs and cut through the skin.

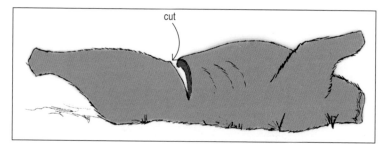

BELOW: Turn the front and rear halves over and cut through the skin down the back bone. Peel back the skin on either side of the cut and use the meat saw to saw each half into quarters.

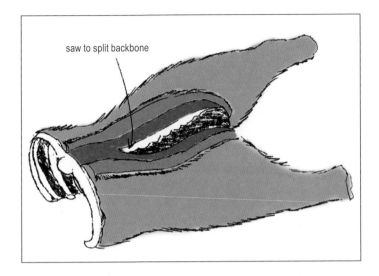

saw to split backbone

BELOW: Wild hogs and javelina are dressed in the same manner as shown in the chapter on pork.

field dressing, skinning, and quartering. Buffalo is done up in the same manner as for beef.

Some states require a bear be taken to a check station whole, or after field dressing. In either case, field dress in the usual manner. In

many instances the bear skin, as well as the unskinned head is saved
to be taken to the taxidermist. Continue the field dressing by cutting to the base of the chin and then make a cut in the hide from each
paw to the centerline cut. Do not skin out the feet pads. Instead skin
around the legs and use a game saw to cut off the feet, leaving the feet
pads attached. By the same token do not attempt to skin out the head,
but skin out around the neck and cut off the head. Bears have quite a
bit of fat, especially on their backs and it's pretty greasy. Any way you
look at it, skinning a bear is a messy chore. The hide can be removed
while the bear is on the ground, or while hoisted from a tree limb,
game pole or other item, although skinning on the ground is fairly
easy, just keep the hide well spread out to keep the meat from touching the ground. Because of the fat, bear hides spoil fairly quickly,
causing the hair to slip. They should be well salted or taken to the
taxidermist as soon as possible.

ABOVE: Bear is a very popular wild game, and prepared properly, good table fare as well.

BELOW: A bear is usually case skinned, leaving the head and feet attached to the pelt for the taxidermist. The carcass is then cut up similar to most other big game.

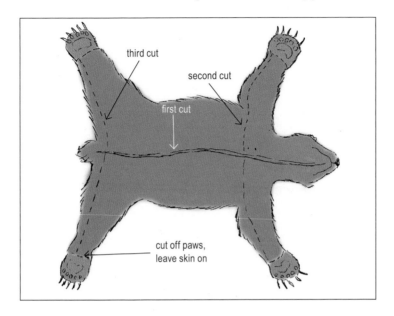

A bear carcass can be taken to camp and cut up similar to deer, hogs or elk, or a larger bear can be cut similar to elk, in either four or seven pieces for transporting. In this case, first cut off the neck, then saw down the spine, finally cutting the two halves into thirds.

Rendering Fat

The old timers often rendered the fat from game animals and used it for cooking. The taste will vary greatly, depending on the species and even the individual animal. To render, cut the fat into small, one-half inch chunks and slowly cook in a large skillet, pouring off the fat as it is rendered. Pour into sterilized fruit jars and keep refrigerated or frozen.

Small Game

Many hunters grew up hunting small game such as rabbits and squirrels. Today small game hunting is still mighty popular. Both rabbits and squirrels make delicious eating.

BELOW: Small game is extremely popular for hunters. Rabbit is very tasty on the table.

Wild cottontails, hares, and even jackrabbits can be field dressed in the same manner as shown in the earlier chapter on dressing tame rabbits. Skinning in the case manner will result in a rabbit skin that can be tanned, and they do make great glove liners. Wild rabbits were common table fare on our Missouri farm in the '50s and I was taught a much simpler and quicker method of dressing them. It takes only seconds, and is a snap—pun intended. Make a cut just through the skin on the back of the rabbit. Grasp the skin on either side of the cut with your hands and simply peel both front and back off, leaving the skin on the head. Cut off the feet, tail and head. Make a cut from the anus and through the rib cage, severing the intestines at the throat. Give the carcass a swing and snap and the intestines will pop right out. Cut the intestines off at the anus and wash the cavity clean.

Caution: Rabbits can become infected with Tularemia, often called rabbit fever, tick fever, deer fly fever, or Pahvant Valley Plague.

BELOW: The simplest method of skinning a rabbit is to make a cut through the skin across the middle of the back. Next grasp the cut hide with both hands and peel the two skin sections off. Eviscerate, cut off head, tail and feet and you're done.

pinch up,
skin and cut

Caused by a bacterium, the disease can be transferred to humans by handling infected rabbits, or inhaling the bacteria on the fur, as well as eating the improperly cooked meat of infected rabbits. Although Tularemia is fairly rare in the United States, be wary of rabbits that appear sick, do not try to run away, or act strangely. The liver of an infected rabbit will have many tiny white spots, and it may also be swollen. The old-timers I grew up with wouldn't hunt rabbits until sometime after a hard freeze, feeling this killed the ticks as well as any sick rabbits. I don't, however, know of any scientific fact proving this. Regardless, to be safe, wear protective rubber or disposable plastic gloves while dressing rabbits.

Squirrels are an extremely popular southern table fare, but how they're prepared depends on the age. Young squirrels can be pan fried much like chicken and are tender and delicious. Older squirrels often take longer cooking to make them less tough and more palatable, and are more commonly used in stews and other means of slow cooking. Before you start dressing or skinning the critters, first determine whether they're young or old-timers. This can be done to some degree by their size, but not necessarily, and grey squirrels will usually be smaller than

BELOW: Squirrel is another popular small game animal, very tasty on the table.

fox squirrels. The testicles on older males will be fairly large. Young males will have less developed testicles. Older females will have dark-ened teats, with the hair worn off around them, evidence of nursing.

BELOW: Young squirrels can be tender, old squirrels tough. It's important to determine the approximate age. The teats on females will be blackened and the hair worn off. Older males have larger testicles.

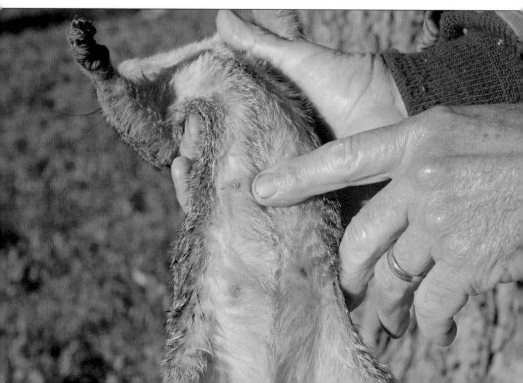

Of all the wild game, squirrels are some of the toughest to skin. Skinning as soon as you can after the animal is killed can make the chore easier. As the carcass cools, the skin "sets" on the animal. Ideally, the squirrel should be skinned within 30 minutes of being killed. If hunting in hot weather it's doubly important to skin and field dress immediately.

Squirrels also present another problem. The hair easily comes off and adheres to the flesh, almost like being glued in place. It can be a real mess trying to pick off the hairs. My good friend and hunting personality Brad Harris showed me a trick to help prevent the prob-

RIGHT: To keep hair off the carcass first dip and soak thoroughly in water.

lem. He suggested soaking before skinning the carcass in water until the hide is thoroughly wet, Brad this to me illustrated on one hunt by dipping the animal in a creek. A bucket of water will also do. Regardless, make sure the hair and skin are soaking wet.

A squirrel can be case skinned, hanging from a tree limb or other item with a string tied around the back ankles. There is, however, an easier way I learned from my granddad many years ago. Sometimes called the Sioux Indian method, it's quick and easy once you get the hang of it. You'll need a good sharp knife.

Place the squirrel on its belly and bend the tail back. Cut from the underside of the tail and next to the anus, completely through the tail bone. Be careful not to cut through the skin on the top of the tail. Make two angled cuts away from the tail on the flanks, leaving a V-shaped section of skin attached to the tail.

BELOW: Place squirrel on its back and cut through the bone of the tail from the underside, but not through the skin on top of the tail.

Place the squirrel on its back and place your foot on the tail and as close to the body as possible. Grasp a hind leg in each hand and slowly pull the carcass up. This will take a bit of effort until the skin begins to pull off. As you pull, the skin will tear apart at the center of the belly. It will peel off the front legs and up to the head. You will have to

ABOVE: Make additional cuts on the flank to leave the tail and a flap of skin.

work you finger under the skin around the legs and between the legs and neck to completely pull the skin off to the front feet.

Stand on the tail and grasp the point of skin on the belly and peel it up. It may take both hands to peel the skin up and over both hind legs to

BELOW: With the squirrel on its back, stand on the tail, grasp a hind leg in each hand, and pull up to peel off the front half of the skin.

BELOW: Use your fingers to work the hide off around the legs and neck area.

BELOW: Use your fingers to work the hide off around the legs and neck area.

the back feet. You should end up with the skin completely off the body, but attached to the feet and head. Cut off the feet, head and tail.

Make a cut through the pelvic bone and up to and through the rib-cage to the neck area, being careful not to cut into the internal organs. Pull out the internal organs and wash carcass thoroughly.

Several other small game critters make passable meals, although some have an "acquired" taste. This includes groundhogs, raccoons, muskrats, beaver, and even opossum. The latter was an occasional dish at my grandparents and I can't say I ever acquired a taste for the critter.

Groundhog is probably the best of the choices. Like squirrel, however, the skin is extremely tough and hard to remove. My dad had a home-made banjo, with the head made of a tanned groundhog skin. It's important to skin and dress immediately after the kill. Groundhog and other critters are normally case skinned, especially if you want to keep the hide. The best method, however, is to first chop off the head and feet with a chopping block and axe or use a very sharp and sturdy hunting knife.

Then slit through the skin up the belly, being careful not to cut into the belly membrane. Make cuts from the belly cut on the inside of the legs to the cut-off feet. Groundhog skin is very tough to remove. You'll have to "flesh" it off or slice it away from the flesh as you gently pull.

BELOW: Stand on the tail, grasp the skin on the rear half, and peel the skin off.

BELOW: Cutting from the anus to the neck, eviscerate the carcass.

Eviscerate in the normal manner. A groundhog can weigh up to 12 or 13 pounds, providing quite a bit of meat. One method of cutting up is to simply debone all the meat, leaving the carcass whole. Or you can cut the carcass into sections. First cut off the front legs with the shoulders. All the furred small game animals have scent glands under their shoulders. Make sure not to cut into these glands, but remove them after removing the shoulders. Cut off the hind legs where they join the belly. Then split into two hind legs and further separate the hind legs at the joint. Cut the backstrap into three sections. Again in most instances the pieces are deboned before cooking. You can, however, parboil the pieces until the meat easily comes off the bone. The meat is usually used in stews, or even stroganoff.

Game Birds

The game birds consist of three separate groups, although field dressing and butchering all three is quite similar. This includes upland game birds, such as dove, quail, pheasant, grouse, prairie chicken, and woodcock. The second category is duck and goose, as well as marsh birds such as rail. The third group is wild turkeys. The three basic methods used for all three groups include breasting, skinning and plucking. The methods used, however, vary somewhat with the species.

As with all wild game, it's extremely important to field dress birds as soon as possible. This is especially important during hot weather, for instance while dove hunting. In this case you may wish to keep a cooler to drop the birds in. Make sure you understand the game laws regarding field dressing of the various species. For instance some states require feet, wings, or other plumage be left on the birds to identify their species and gender.

Breasting is usually the simplest method. Breasting is often used for ducks and geese as well as wild turkeys. Breasting is a common method for doves.

Cleaning doves is quick and easy, but somewhat messy as the feathers tend to come out quite easily and float around everywhere,

RIGHT: Game birds such as this pheasant are extremely popular among hunters.

LEFT: Different methods are often used for the different birds. Doves are usually dressed by simply twisting off the wings, popping out and skinning the breast.

creating somewhat of a mess. The feathers also stick to your hands. Many retrievers simply will not pick up doves because of the mouthful of feathers. Simply push the fingertips of one hand into the soft spot below the point of the breastbone and bend upward. In most instances you can simply snap the breast free. Or, you can use a sharp knife or game shears to separate the breast from the wing bones, but it's usually not necessary. Peel off the small piece of skin left on the breast. Place the breasts in a pan of cold water and pour off any feathers that float to the surface. Snapping off all the breasts, peeling off the skin and feathers and then washing all the cleaned breast is the best tactic, rather than doing the individual breasts.

Breasting can also be used with other game birds. Waterfowl, including ducks and geese, as well as wild turkeys and sometimes pheasants are breasted. Part of the reason is the meat on the wings and legs is often tougher. Breasting is often the best choice on older birds, regardless of the species. Quite often the smaller diver ducks are also breasted. With generous goose limits breasting is a great

LEFT: Game birds are, waterfowl and turkey are sometimes breasted with the two halves of the breast removed, and the carcass discarded.

tactic for these birds, especially snows and blues. Then grind the breast meat into delicious summer sausage. Breasting is quick and easy and results in two fillets of meat ready to pan fry or cook in other methods. Lay the bird on its back and using a sharp boning or fillet knife, slice through the skin only on the center line of the breast, from the tip of the breastbone to the throat area. Use your fingers to pull the skin back off the breast and down the sides from the legs to the wings.

Locate the sharp breastbone and using the boning knife slice down one side of the breastbone, starting at the top of the breast and proceeding downward. Continue to follow the bone with the knife blade. As you make the slice with one hand, pull the meat away with the opposite, exposing the breastbone and rib cage as you make the cut. This should loosen all but the upper portion of the breast at the wing joint. Turn your knife around and cut upward from your first cut allowing the knife blade to follow the Y-bone to the wing. Finally cut through the tough muscle connecting the breast to the wing bone, and you have a nice, clean breast fillet. Repeat these steps for the opposite breast piece.

BELOW: Begin the breasting method by cutting through and peeling back the skin from the breast.

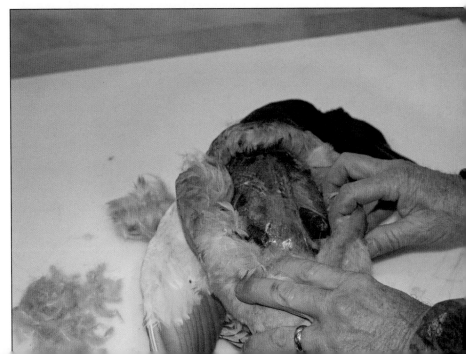

BELOW: Using a boning knife, slice down along one side of the breastbone.

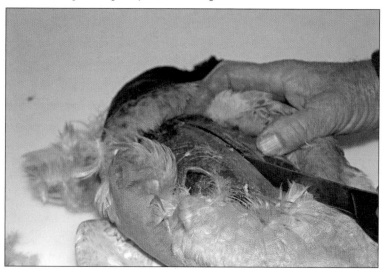

BELOW: Following the breastbone and rib cage, continue cutting and pulling the breast piece away as you go.

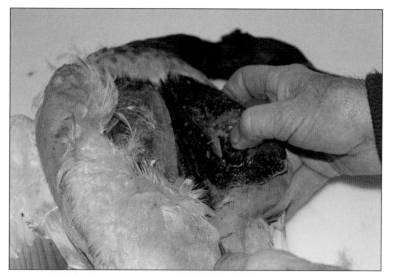

You can also create a "bone-in" breast piece on smaller birds, such as rails, snipe or woodcock, somewhat similar to breasting out a dove. Again peel the skin away to expose the breast. If the bird has not been field dressed, cut an opening below the point of the breast,

BELOW: Turn the knife around and cut along the Y-bone severing the tough muscle connecting the breast to the wing bone.

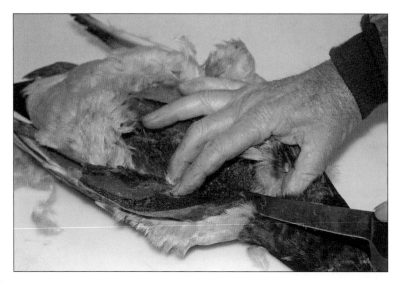

BELOW: Breasting is an excellent tactic for big geese, especially snows and blues.

insert your fingers and pull the entire breast back to pop it away from the rest of the carcass. Cut the breast away from the wing joint with a knife or game shears and then continue to pull the breast back until you can cut it free of the skin and muscles of the neck. This makes a nice, but small piece for baking.

Breasting is often the best option for a big and old tom turkey as well. Proceed in the same manner as described previously, with a couple of exceptions. First remove the beard if a tom. Cut the beard out, or grasp it at its base and holding the skin with your other hand, simply pull the beard loose. You will also have to cut the breast pieces away from the "sponge" or crop area in front of the breast.

Skinning is a common method of preparing game birds that have extremely tender skin that tears easily if they are plucked. A good example is bobwhite quail. Skinning some birds is easy, others tougher.

Skinning a quail is quite easy. Unless the weather is hot, these birds are not normally field dressed until after they are skinned. In hot weather eviscerate immediately after they are killed. To skin before eviscerating, remove the head. This can be done by simply pulling and twisting, or use game shears. The wings can also be twisted off, or use a sharp knife or game shears to remove them close to the body. The cut ends of wing bones can be sharp so remove with care. Remove the bottom portions of the legs by first bending backward to snap the knee joint. Using a sharp knife or game shears, remove the bottom portion of the legs at the "knee" joint. Holding the bird with its belly up, pinch the skin up at the base of the breast and peel it off. Continue peeling off the remainder of the skin and pull off the crop. If the bird hasn't been eviscerated in the field, pull up the breast and push your finger through the belly skin. Pull out the entrails down to the pelvic bone. Snap the pelvic bone to separate the legs and cut off the entrails, vent and tail with a sharp knife or game shears. The carcass can be cooked whole, cut into two halves down the breast and leg, or the whole leg section twisted off the breast creating two pieces.

RIGHT: Breasting is also a good choice for an old, tough gobbler.

BELOW: Smaller birds such as bobwhite quail are often skinned. First twist off the head and wings, then start at the breast and peel the skin off. Finally remove the feet and eviscerate.

LEFT: Almost all game birds, including upland birds, can be skinned.

Other upland game birds, such as grouse and pheasant can also be skinned in the same manner. The legs, head and wings are first removed. A game shear makes this chore much easier, especially on the larger birds. Remember to leave identifying features as required by state law for transportation. Pull back enough feathers to reveal the skin and cut just through the skin starting at the vent and up to the neck. Peel the skin and feathers back and pull off the entire cape, skin, feathers and all. When you get to the tail, cut it off, but leave it attached to the cape. Remove the crop or craw. Eviscerate in the same manner as described previously. Rinse the bird to remove any blood and/or feathers.

Waterfowl can also be skinned and is a popular method of dressing. Waterfowl, however, tends to be dry and dry out even worse when cooked in many methods with the skin off. When removing the wings bend them back away from the body and cut free with a knife. Remove the skin in the same manner. The skin will peel off fairly easily from the belly and legs, but tends to stick at two places on the upper back.

BELOW: Waterfowl and turkey can also be skinned. First step is to cut off the head, feet, wings, and tail.

BE;LOW: Pull back enough feathers on the belly to reveal the skin, then cut through the skin from the point of the breast to the neck.

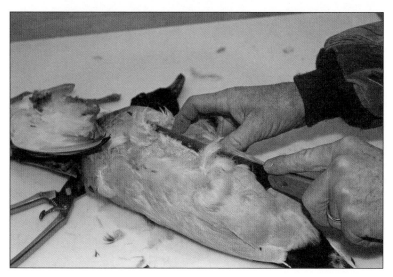

A wild turkey can also be skinned in this manner, but can be somewhat awkward to handle due to their size. I prefer to hang turkeys by one foot from a tree limb or other source for skinning.

BELOW: Then simply peel off the skin, starting with the breast, then the legs, sides, and finally the back.

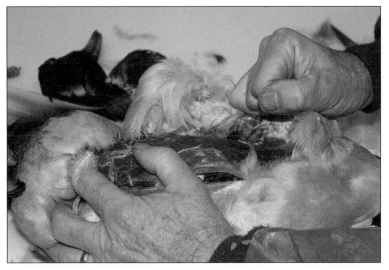

BELOW: It's often best to pluck small game birds and waterfowl instead of breasting. Dry plucking is the most common method.

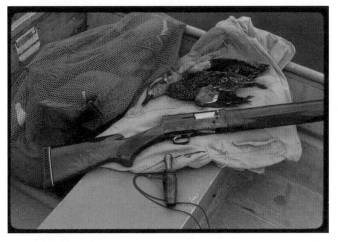

Almost all game birds can also be plucked. Plucking is the preferred method for some species, as well as some cooking methods. Birds can be dry plucked or wet plucked. Field-dressed birds must be dry plucked. Wet-plucked birds are best left whole. I prefer to leave the legs, head and wings on the bird for dry plucking as this gives me

BELOW: Continue pulling out feathers around the rest of the carcass.

BELOW: Pull out the pin-feathers and singe off the hairs.

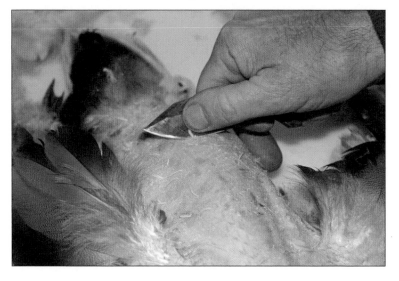

more hand holds for turning and holding the bird. Dry plucking can be anywhere from an easy chore to a tedious job, depending on the bird and size. Dry plucking a grouse or teal is fairly easy. Dry plucking a big old honker or tom turkey can be work and takes quite a bit of time.

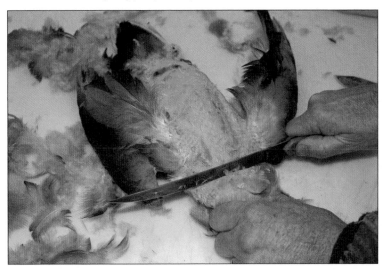

Start the plucking on the belly pulling the feathers back toward the head, and continue plucking the legs down to the joints and around the sides and back. The back is the hardest to pluck, as the feathers are larger and more embedded. Use a propane blow torch to singe off the hair-feathers. Pull out any pin feathers with a sharp knife and your thumb or a pair of pliers. If dry plucking waterfowl, keep a large paper sack to hold the feathers as they tend to fly everywhere. If you dry pluck a lot of waterfowl, you will probably want to consider a plucking machine. Once the bird has been plucked, eviscerate and remove head, wings and bottom portions of the legs.

Most birds can also be wet-plucked, even a big wild turkey or goose. This requires heating water in a large pot, and it's somewhat difficult to get a pot large enough. My friend Dr. Jerry Thies uses an old cooler, pouring pans of boiling water in it to dip the larger birds. Once the bird has been scalded in the hot water, pluck in the same manner as dry plucking. For more information on wet plucking, refer to the poultry chapter.

Waterfowl are also sometimes plucked using the wax method. I've tried it and it works, but it is also a bit of work and doesn't do as well on larger geese. Paraffin wax is heated using a double boiler method, but caution must be used as wax can catch on fire. The bird is dipped in the melted wax, immediately wrapped in newspaper and allowed to cool. Then the newspaper, wax and feathers are all removed.

BELOW: Fish may be dressed in a wide variety of ways.

Fish

Fish have been a staple of mankind since our beginning and are not only still a very important food source, but good for you as well. Fish may be dressed in any number of ways and of course, cooked in a wide variety of methods as well. The method of dressing depends on the species and the preferred method of cooking. The basic market forms of fish can also be created by the home butcher as well. These include dressed, or eviscerated and with the head on. Dressed with the head off, dressed with the fins, tail and head removed. Skinned, left with skin on, and scaled. Other forms include dressed and cut into steaks, dressed and cut into chunks, and filleted creating two fillets. Almost all species can be dressed in any of these methods.

Trout and the salmonoids are often cooked dressed and with the head on, or dressed and with the head removed. The skin is normally

BELOW: The market cuts of most fish are shown below.

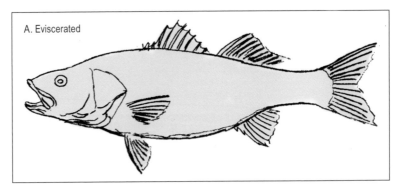

A. Eviscerated

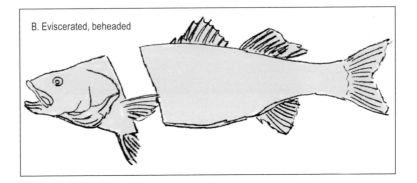

B. Eviscerated, beheaded

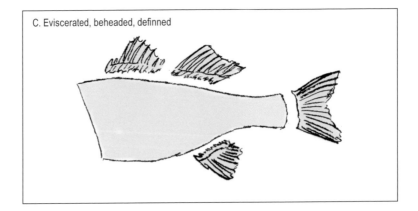

C. Eviscerated, beheaded, definned

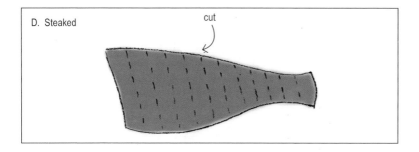

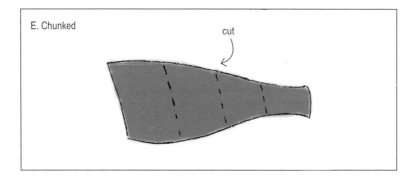

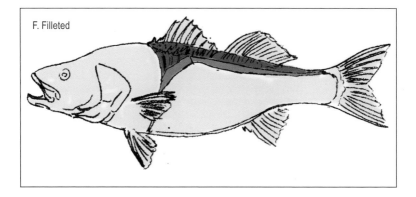

left on for these fish as it retains the moisture and keeps the delicate flesh from falling apart.

Panfish such as bluegill, white bass and crappie can be gutted, the head removed and the scales removed with a fish scaler. Some

LEFT: Trout and the salmonids may be dressed with the head on or off.

folks like to leave on the tail and fins, but I prefer to remove the fins and peel off the skin on the smaller fish. Larger bluegill and crappie are more often filleted. There's not much size to bluegill fillets, but they're my wife's favorite. White bass are most often filleted. The red

BELOW: Insert fillet knife into fish's belly at the vent.

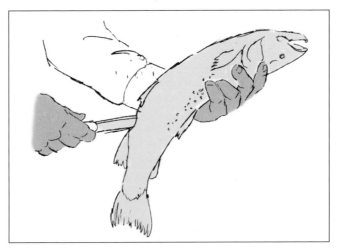

BELOW: Slice to the throat.

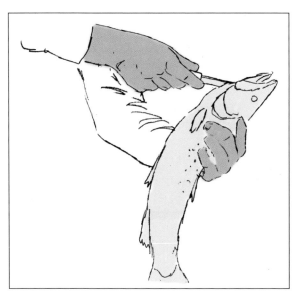

BELOW: Slip the knife under the fish's tongue and make an upward stroke.

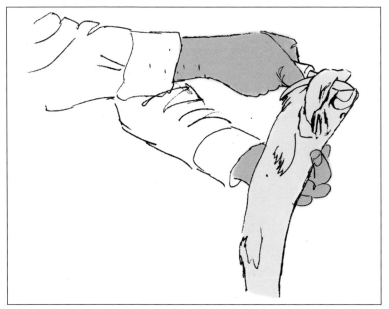

BELOW: Insert fingers into the slit made under the fish's tongue.

BELOW: Pull down quickly to remove gills and entrails.

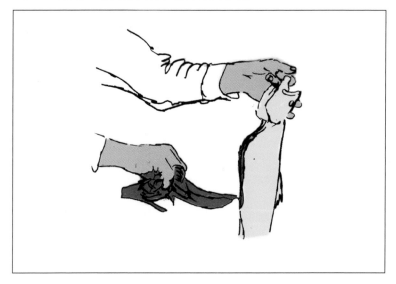

BELOW: With the trout on its back, cut from the vent to the throat just through the skin.

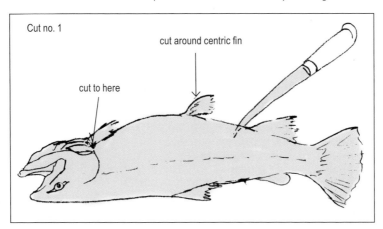

BELOW: Turn the trout back on its belly and cut behind the head to the backbone, then cut behind the gills on both sides.

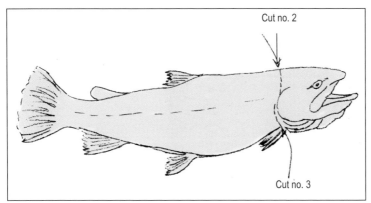

BELOW: Simply snap the head downward, then pull away head and entrails.

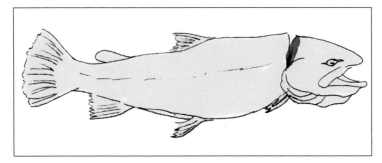

BELOW: Panfish such as bluegill, and others are often dressed by simply removing the head, fins, tail, and entrails, then scaling.

BELOW: With the fish lying on its side, use the tip of a fillet knife to slice around the fins on the back and belly.

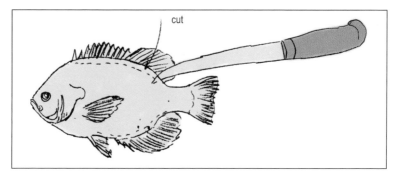

BELOW: With fish pliers, pull out the fins, cut off the head and eviscerate. Fish can be skinned and the tail cut off, or the scales can be removed.

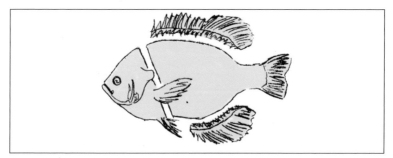

LEFT: Filleting is the easiest method for many species, especially larger fish, resulting in a boneless piece of meat.

streak down the middle of the side must be cut away as it provides an off flavor.

Largemouth, smallmouth, Kentucky, and striped bass can be gutted, fins, tail and skin removed and the fish left whole for baking.

BELOW: Cut behind the head down to the backbone and ribs.

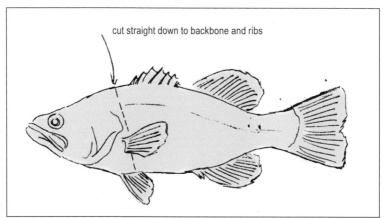

cut straight down to backbone and ribs

BELOW: Turn the fillet knife sideways and cut following the backbone and through the ribs almost to the tail.

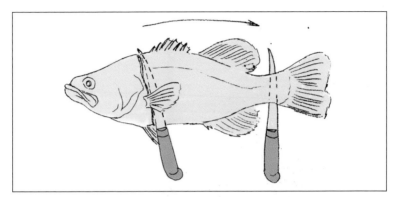

BELOW: Flop the fillet, still attached at the tail, and cut between the skin and meat.

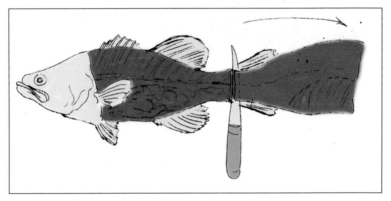

BELOW: Cut the rib section away, leaving the boneless fillet. Cut the other side in the same manner.

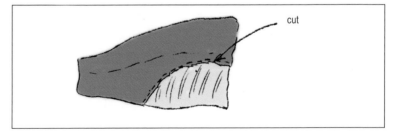

LEFT: Catfish are some of the toughest fish to dress. The most common method is to skin, cut out fins, remove tail and head, and eviscerate. Smaller cats are left whole or filleted; larger cats are cut into steaks or chunks.

The most common method for these fish, however, is to fillet them. The red streak on striped bass should also be removed and larger striped bass can be cut into chunks or steaks.

Although one of the most popular and tasty fish, the catfish family are somewhat harder to dress. They are usually eviscerated, the

BELOW: To skin a catfish, cut through the skin around the back of the head. Make a cut on both sides of the fins along the entire back and belly.

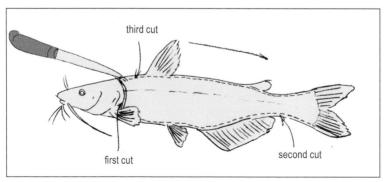

third cut

first cut

second cut

BELOW: Using fish skinning pliers peel off the skin. Slippery catfish can be placed on a towel for easier holding.

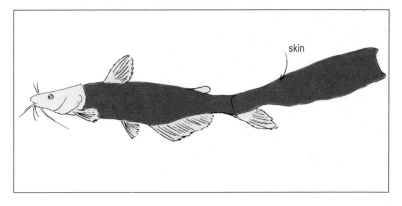

BELOW: Pull out the fins with fish skinning pliers or clip off with tin snips. Eviscerate then remove the head and tail.

head, fins, tail, and skin removed. Smaller cats can be cooked whole, medium size cats can be left whole or filleted. Large cats are cut into chunks or steaks.

Northern pike are most commonly filleted, and it takes a bit of extra work because of the tiny Y-bones.

Walleye may be eviscerated, head, tail and skin removed and cooked whole, chunked or they may also be filleted. I prefer the latter in most instances because even a smaller size walleye provides a nice long filet.

RIGHT: Saltwater fish are a delicacy to many, with the different species offering a variety of tastes.

LEFT: Inshore species are normally filleted.

ABOVE: Offshore species may be filleted, cut into steaks, or chunked, depending on the species and size.

BELOW: The larger saltwater species are usually cut into steaks or chunked.

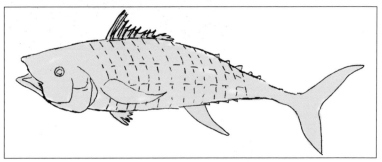

The rough fish, such as carp, buffalo, and suckers were a favorite of my dad. These fish are beheaded, the tail and fins removed and the skin pulled off. The latter is somewhat difficult on larger fish and they are often cooked whole or chunked. The problem is these fish are filled with tiny bones. My family preferred to chunk them up and preserve them by pressure canning which softens the bones making them edible. They're quite tasty, resembling canned salmon and make great "cakes."

The various salt water fish species are also dressed in the standard market forms, but the variety of species sometimes require somewhat different tactics. Most inshore species are filleted, although some are dressed leaving the fish whole and baked, chunked or cut into steaks. The larger off-shore species are dressed and cut into steaks or chunked, leaving the skin on some and removing the skin on others.

Conclusion

MANY FOLKS ARE dubious about taking on home butchering, meat cutting, and meat preparation. I hope reading this book will alleviate some of these fears. Like many life skills, such as gardening, raising livestock, and canning and preserving food, home butchering can be very satisfying and extremely helpful. Learning and practicing any skill is satisfying, but preparing your own food also provides two other advantages: saving money and knowing where and how your food is grown and prepared. These days meat most commonly comes prepackaged in plastic containers at the grocery store, and most folks have no way of connecting the packaged products with the real thing—meat from birds and animals. This is especially so of the younger generations.

Home butchering of livestock or hunting and butchering of wild game is a real time connection to the cycle of life. If you're a hunter, knowing how to field dress, butcher, and prepare meat is an invaluable and money-saving skill. Many years ago when I field dressed and butchered my first deer I had no idea what I was doing, and since deer weren't available on our farm when I was growing up, there was also no one to teach me. I had to learn the hard way. Over the years I refined my deer field-dressing and butchering skills and became the "go-to" fellow in the neighborhood when someone killed their first deer. I enjoy passing these skills along to others, including numerous young first-time deer hunters. The skills I eventually learned were also well appreciated on a mountaintop in Idaho when it came time to field dress my first elk. Hopefully, you've learned in this book some of the hard-earned but untraditional methods I've worked out, especially for dressing game, such as deer.

One of the keys to learning any skill is to take things one step at a time, learn how to do the simple stuff, and then proceed to the more complicated chores. This also goes for the tools needed for butchering. Acquire a few tools as you need them. Most butchering tools, however, will more than keep their value throughout the years.

Growing up on a farm in the '40s and '50s, I learned many of these skills from my parents, grandparents, and other relatives. Even after leaving the farm and living in cities for a number of years—earning my living as an editor, among other jobs—my wife Joan and I continued to return to participate in our family farm "butchering days." With the publication of my first book in 1971, Joan and I left the city for good, bought a rundown farm in the Ozarks, and began a "back to the farm basics" lifestyle with our three kids as we grew our own livestock (which we then butchered), raised a giant garden, and started an orchard. We've continued over the years to write magazine articles and books.

This book is actually the last published in a series of life-skills books written for Skyhorse Publishing. The series takes you through the entire process, from field dressing and butchering, to the final steps such as making sausage and smoking and curing meats. The other two books include: *The Complete Jerky Book: How to Dry, Cure, and Preserve Everything from Venison to Turkey* and *The Joy of Smoking and Salt Curing*. This book takes you through curing your own hams and bacon, as well as how to smoke and cure meat, fish, game and a section on hot smoking with recipes. *The Complete Guide to Sausage Making* includes mastering the art of homemade bratwurst, bologna, pepperoni, salami, breakfast sausage, and more. I also added another book, to the life-skills line: *The Ultimate Guide to Growing Your Own Food: Save Money, Live Better, and Enjoy Life with Food from Your Garden or Orchard*.

Index

Notes

FEEL FREE TO use the following pages to jot down your own notes on home butchering, whether they are lessons learned from experience, tips from friends and family, or plans for recipes to try soon.